Toronto Blue Jays 2021

A Baseball Companion

Edited by Steven Goldman and Bret Sayre

Baseball Prospectus

Craig Brown, Associate Editor
Robert Au, Harry Pavlidis and Amy Pircher, Statistics Editors

Library of Congress Cataloging-in-Publication Data:
paperback
ISBN-13: 978-1-950716-81-4

Project Credits
Cover Design: Ginny Searle
Interior Design and Production: Amy Pircher, Robert Au
Layout: Amy Pircher, Robert Au

Baseball icon courtesy of Uberux, from https://www.shareicon.net/author/uberux

Ballpark diagram courtesy of Lou Spirito/THIRTY81 Project, https://thirty81project.com/

Manufactured in the United States of America
10 9 8 7 6 5 4 3 2 1

Table of Contents

Part 1: Team Analysis

Part 2: Player Analysis

Part 3: Featured Articles

Statistical Introduction

Sports are, fundamentally, a blend of athletic endeavor and storytelling. Baseball, like any other sport, tells its stories in so many ways: in the arc of a game from the stands or a season from the box scores, in photos, or even in numbers. At Baseball Prospectus, we understand that statistics don't replace observation or any of baseball's stories, but complement everything else that makes the game so much fun.

What stats help us with is with patterns and precision, variance and value. This book can help you learn things you may not see from watching a game or hundred, whether it's the path of a career over time or the breadth of the entire MLB. We'd also never ask you to choose between our numbers and the experience of viewing a game from the cheap seats or the comfort of your home; our publication combines running the numbers with observations and wisdom from some of the brightest minds we can find. But if you *do* want to learn more about the numbers beyond what's on the backs of player jerseys, let us help explain.

Offense

We've revised our methodology for determining batting value. Long-time readers of the book will notice that we've retired True Average in favor of a new metric: Deserved Runs Created Plus (DRC+). Developed by Jonathan Judge and our stats team, this statistic measures everything a player does at the plate–reaching base, hitting for power, making outs, and moving runners over–and puts it on a scale where 100 equals league-average performance. A DRC+ of 150 is terrific, a DRC+ of 100 is average and a DRC+ of 75 means you better be an excellent defender.

DRC+ also does a better job than any of our previous metrics in taking contextual factors into account. The model adjusts for how the park affects performance, but also for things like the talent of the opposing pitcher, value of different types of batted-ball events, league, temperature and other factors. It's able to describe a player's expected offensive contribution than any other statistic we've found over the years, and also does a better job of predicting future performance as well.

The other aspect of run-scoring is baserunning, which we quantify using Baserunning Runs. BRR not only records the value of stolen bases (or getting caught in the act), but also accounts for all the stuff that doesn't show up on the back of a baseball card: a runner's ability to go first to third on a single, or advance on a fly ball.

Defense

Where offensive value is *relatively* easy to identify and understand, defensive value is ... not. Over the past dozen years, the sabermetric community has focused mostly on stats based on zone data: a real-live human person records the type of batted ball and estimated landing location, and models are created that give expected outs. From there, you can compare fielders' actual outs to those expected ones. Simple, right?

Unfortunately, zone data has two major issues. First, zone data is recorded by commercial data providers who keep the raw data private unless you pay for it. (All the statistics we build in this book and on our website use public data as inputs.) That hurts our ability to test assumptions or duplicate results. Second, over the years it has become apparent that there's quite a bit of "noise" in zone-based fielding analysis. Sometimes the conclusions drawn from zone data don't hold up to scrutiny, and sometimes the different data provided by different providers don't look anything alike, giving wildly different results. Sometimes the hard-working professional stringers or scorers might unknowingly inflict unconscious bias into the mix: for example good fielders will often be credited with more expected outs despite the data, and ballparks with high press boxes tend to score more line drives than ones with a lower press box.

Enter our Fielding Runs Above Average (FRAA). For most positions, FRAA is built from play-by-play data, which allows us to avoid the subjectivity found in many other fielding metrics. The idea is this: count how many fielding plays are made by a given player and compare that to expected plays for an average fielder at their position (based on pitcher ground ball tendencies and batter handedness). Then we adjust for park and base-out situations.

When it comes to catchers, our methodology is a little different thanks to the laundry list of responsibilities they're tasked with beyond just, well, catching and throwing the ball. By now you've probably heard about "framing" or the art of making umpires more likely to call balls outside the strike zone for strikes. To put this into one tidy number, we incorporate pitch tracking data (for the years it exists) and adjust for important factors like pitcher, umpire, batter and home-field advantage using a mixed-model approach. This grants us a number for how many strikes the catcher is personally adding to (or subtracting from) his pitchers' performance ... which we then convert to runs added or lost using linear weights.

Framing is one of the biggest parts of determining catcher value, but we also take into account blocking balls from going past, whether a scorer deems it a passed ball or a wild pitch. We use a similar approach—one that really benefits from the pitch tracking data that tells us what ends up in the dirt and what doesn't. We also include a catcher's ability to prevent stolen bases and how well they field balls in play, and *finally* we come up with our FRAA for catchers.

Pitching

Both pitching and fielding make up the half of baseball that isn't run scoring: run prevention. Separating pitching from fielding is a tough task, and most recent pitching analysis has branched off from Voros McCracken's famous (and controversial) statement, "There is little if any difference among major-league pitchers in their ability to prevent hits on balls hit in the field of play." The research of the analytic community has validated this to some extent, and there are a host of "defense-independent" pitching measures that have been developed to try and extract the effect of the defense behind a hurler from the pitcher's work.

Our solution to this quandary is Deserved Run Average (DRA), our core pitching metric. DRA seeks to evaluate a pitcher's performance, much like earned run average (ERA), the tried-and-true pitching stat you've seen on every baseball broadcast or box score from the past century, but it's very different. To start, DRA takes an event-by-event look at what the pitchers does, and adjusts the value of that event based on different environmental factors like park, batter, catcher, umpire, base-out situation, run differential, inning, defense, home field advantage, pitcher role and temperature. That mixed model gives us a pitcher's expected contribution, similar to what we do for our DRC+ model for hitters and FRAA model for catchers. (Oh, and we also consider the pitcher's effect on basestealing and on balls getting past the catcher.)

DRA is set to the scale of runs allowed per nine innings (RA9) instead of ERA, which makes DRA's scale slightly higher than ERA's. Because of this, for ease of use, we're supplying DRA-, which is much easier for the reader to parse. As with DRC+, DRA- is an "index" stat, meaning instead of using some arbitrary and shifting number to denote what's "good," average is always 100. The reason that it uses a minus rather than a plus is because like ERA, a lower number is better. Therefore a 75 DRA- describes a performance 25 percent better than average, whereas a 150 DRA- means that either a pitcher is getting extremely lucky with their results, or getting ready to try a new pitch.

Since the last time you picked up an edition of this book, we've also made a few minor changes to DRA to make it better. Recent research into "tunneling"—the act of throwing consecutive pitches that appear similar from a batter's point of view until after the swing decision point–data has given us a new contextual factor to account for in DRA: plate distance. This refers to the distance between successive pitches as they approach the plate, and while it has a smaller effect than factors like velocity or whiff rate, it still can help explain pitcher strikeout rate in our model.

Recently Added Descriptive Statistics

Returning to our 2021 edition of the book are a few figures which recently appeared. These numbers may be a little bit more familiar to those of you who have spent some time investigating baseball statistics.

Fastball Percentage

Our fastball percentage (FA%) statistic measures how frequently a pitcher throws a pitch classified as a "fastball," measured as a percentage of overall pitches thrown. We qualify three types of fastballs:

1. The traditional four-seam fastball;
2. The two-seam fastball or sinker;
3. "Hard cutters," which are pitches that have the movement profile of a cut fastball and are used as the pitcher's primary offering or in place of a more traditional fastball.

For example, a pitcher with a FA% of 67 throws any combination of these three pitches about two-thirds of the time.

Whiff Rate

Everybody loves a swing and a miss, and whiff rate (Whiff%) measures how frequently pitchers induce a swinging strike. To calculate Whiff%, we add up all the pitches thrown that ended with a swinging strike, then divide that number by a pitcher's total pitches thrown. Most often, high whiff rates correlate with high strikeout rates (and overall effective pitcher performance).

Called Strike Probability

Called Strike Probability (CSP) is a number that represents the likelihood that all of a pitcher's pitches will be called a strike while controlling for location, pitcher and batter handedness, umpire and count. Here's how it works: on each pitch, our model determines how many times (out of 100) that a similar pitch was called for a strike given those factors mentioned above, and when normalized for each batter's strike zone. Then we average the CSP for all pitches thrown by a pitcher in a season, and that gives us the yearly CSP percentage you see in the stats boxes.

As you might imagine, pitchers with a higher CSP are more likely to work in the zone, where pitchers with a lower CSP are likely locating their pitches outside the normal strike zone, for better or for worse.

Projections

Many of you aren't turning to this book just for a look at what a player has done, but for a look at what a player is going to do: the PECOTA projections. PECOTA, initially developed by Nate Silver (who has moved on to greater fame as a political analyst), consists of three parts:

1. Major-league equivalencies, which use minor-league statistics to project how a player will perform in the major leagues;

2. Baseline forecasts, which use weighted averages and regression to the mean to estimate a player's current true talent level; and

3. Aging curves, which uses the career paths of comparable players to estimate how a player's statistics are likely to change over time.

With all those important things covered, let's take a look at what's in the book this year.

Team Prospectus

Most of this book is composed of team chapters, with one for each of the 30 major-league franchises. On the first page of each chapter, you'll see a box that contains some of the key statistics for each team as well as a very inviting stadium diagram.

We start with the team name, their unadjusted 2020 win-loss record, and their divisional ranking. Beneath that are a host of other team statistics. **Pythag** presents an adjusted 2020 winning percentage, calculated by taking runs scored per game (**RS/G**) and runs allowed per game (**RA/G**) for the team, and running them through a version of Bill James' Pythagorean formula that was refined and improved by David Smyth and Brandon Heipp. (The formula is called "Pythagenpat," which is equally fun to type and to say.)

Next up is **DRC+**, described earlier, to indicate the overall hitting ability of the team either above or below league-average. Run prevention on the pitching side is covered by **DRA** (also mentioned earlier) and another metric: Fielding Independent Pitching (**FIP**), which calculates another ERA-like statistic based on strikeouts, walks, and home runs recorded. Defensive Efficiency Rating (**DER**) tells us the percentage of balls in play turned into outs for the team, and is a quick fielding shorthand that rounds out run prevention.

After that, we have several measures related to roster composition, as opposed to on-field performance. **B-Age** and **P-Age** tell us the average age of a team's batters and pitchers, respectively. **Payroll** is the combined team payroll for all on-field players, and Doug Pappas' Marginal Dollars per Marginal Win (**M$/MW**) tells us how much money a team spent to earn production above replacement level.

Next to each of these stats, we've listed each team's MLB rank in that category from first to 30th. In this, first always indicates a positive outcome and 30th a negative outcome, except in the case of salary—first is highest.

After the franchise statistics, we share a few items about the team's home ballpark. There's the aforementioned diagram of the park's dimensions (including distances to the outfield wall), a graphic showing the height of the wall from the left-field pole to the right-field pole, and a table showing three-year park factors for the stadium. The park factors are displayed as indexes where 100 is average, 110 means that the park inflates the statistic in question by 10 percent, and 90 means that the park deflates the statistic in question by 10 percent.

On the second page of each team chapter, you'll find three graphs. The first is **Payroll History** and helps you see how the team's payroll has compared to the MLB and divisional average payrolls over time. Payroll figures are current as of January 1, 2021; with so many free agents still unsigned as of this writing, the final 2021 figure will likely be significantly different for many teams. (In the meantime, you can always find the most current data at Baseball Prospectus' Cot's Baseball Contracts page.)

The second graph is **Future Commitments** and helps you see the team's future outlays, if any.

The third graph is **Farm System Ranking** and displays how the Baseball Prospectus prospect team has ranked the organization's farm system since 2007.

After the graphs, we have a **Personnel** section that lists many of the important decision-makers and upper-level field and operations staff members for the franchise, as well as any former Baseball Prospectus staff members who are currently part of the organization. (In very rare circumstances, someone might be on both lists!)

Position Players

After all that information and a thoughtful bylined essay covering each team, we present our player comments. These are also bylined, but due to frequent franchise shifts during the offseason, our bylines are more a rough guide than a perfect accounting of who wrote what.

Each player is listed with the major-league team that employed him as of early January 2021. If a player changed teams after that point via free agency, trade, or any other method, you'll be able to find them in the chapter for their previous squad.

As an example, take a look at the player comment for Padres shortstop Fernando Tatis Jr.: the stat block that accompanies his written comment is at the top of this page. First we cover biographical information (age is as of June 30, 2021) before moving onto the stats themselves. Our statistic columns include standard identifying information like **YEAR, TEAM, LVL** (level of affiliated play) and **AGE** before getting into the numbers. Next, we provide raw, untranslated

Fernando Tatis Jr. SS

Born: 01/02/99   Age: 22   Bats: R   Throws: R
Height: 6'3"   Weight: 217   Origin: International Free Agent, 2015

YEAR	TEAM	LVL	AGE	PA	R	2B	3B	HR	RBI	BB	K	SB	CS	AVG/OBP/SLG
2018	SA	AA	19	394	77	22	4	16	43	33	109	16	5	.286/.355/.507
2019	SD	MLB	20	372	61	13	6	22	53	30	110	16	6	.317/.379/.590
2020	SD	MLB	21	257	50	11	2	17	45	27	61	11	3	.277/.366/.571
2021 FS	SD	MLB	22	600	95	24	4	31	81	50	165	17	8	.263/.331/.499
2021 DC	SD	MLB	22	628	100	25	4	32	85	53	173	19	8	.263/.331/.499

Comparables: Darryl Strawberry, Bo Bichette, Ronald Acuña Jr.

YEAR	TEAM	LVL	AGE	PA	DRC+	BABIP	BRR	FRAA	WARP
2018	SA	AA	19	394	136	.370	3.0	SS(83): -1.9	2.4
2019	SD	MLB	20	372	118	.410	7.1	SS(83): 0.9	3.4
2020	SD	MLB	21	257	126	.306	0.7	SS(57): -5.5	0.9
2021 FS	SD	MLB	22	600	126	.318	1.7	SS -1	3.9
2021 DC	SD	MLB	22	628	126	.318	1.8	SS -1	4.0

numbers like you might find on the back of your dad's baseball cards: **PA** (plate appearances), **R** (runs), **2B** (doubles), **3B** (triples), **HR** (home runs), **RBI** (runs batted in), **BB** (walks), **K** (strikeouts), **SB** (stolen bases) and **CS** (caught stealing).

Following the basic stats is **Whiff%** (whiff rate), which denotes how often, when a batter swings, he fails to make contact with the ball. Another way to think of this number is an inverse of a hitter's contact rate.

Next, we have unadjusted "slash" statistics: **AVG** (batting average), **OBP** (on-base percentage) and **SLG** (slugging percentage). Following the slash line is **DRC+** (Deserved Runs Created Plus), which we described earlier as total offensive expected contribution compared to the league average.

BABIP (batting average on balls in play) tells us how often a ball in play fell for a hit, and can help us identify whether a batter may have been lucky or not … but note that high BABIPs also tend to follow the great hitters of our time, as well as speedy singles hitters who put the ball on the ground.

The next item is **BRR** (Baserunning Runs), which covers all of a player's baserunning accomplishments including (but not limited to) swiped bags and failed attempts. Next is **FRAA** (Fielding Runs Above Average), which also includes the number of games previously played at each position noted in parentheses. Multi-position players have only their two most frequent positions listed here, but their total FRAA number reflects all positions played.

Our last column here is **WARP** (Wins Above Replacement Player). WARP estimates the total value of a player, which means for hitters it takes into account hitting runs above average (calculated using the DRC+ model), BRR and FRAA. Then, it makes an adjustment for positions played and gives the player a credit for plate appearances based upon the difference between "replacement level"—which is derived from the quality of players added to a team's roster after the start of the season–and the league average.

The final line just below the stats box is **PECOTA** data, which is discussed further in a following section.

Catchers

Catchers are a special breed, and thus they have earned their own separate box which displays some of the defensive metrics that we've built just for them. As an example, let's check out Yasmani Grandal.

YEAR	TEAM	P. COUNT	FRM RUNS	BLK RUNS	THRW RUNS	TOT RUNS
2018	LAD	16816	15.7	0.8	0.1	16.5
2019	MIL	18740	19.4	1.8	-0.1	21.1
2020	CHW	4830	3.7	0.3	-0.2	3.8
2021	CHW	14430	16.7	-0.6	1.0	17.1
2021	CHW	14430	16.7	0.4	1.0	18.0

The **YEAR** and **TEAM** columns match what you'd find in the other stat box. **P. COUNT** indicates the number of pitches thrown while the catcher was behind the plate, including swinging strikes, fouls and balls in play. **FRM RUNS** is the total run value the catcher provided (or cost) his team by influencing the umpire to call strikes where other catchers did not. **BLK RUNS** expresses the total run value above or below average for the catcher's ability to prevent wild pitches and passed balls. **THRW RUNS** is calculated using a similar model as the previous two statistics, and it measures a catcher's ability to throw out basestealers but also to dissuade them from testing his arm in the first place. It takes into account factors like the pitcher (including his delivery and pickoff move) and baserunner (who could be as fast as Billy Hamilton or as slow as Yonder Alonso). **TOT RUNS** is the sum of all of the previous three statistics.

Pitchers

Let's give our pitchers a turn, using 2020 AL Cy Young winner Shane Bieber as our example. Take a look at his stat block: the first line and the **YEAR**, **TEAM**, **LVL** and **AGE** columns are the same as in the position player example earlier.

Here too, we have a series of columns that display raw, unadjusted statistics compiled by the pitcher over the course of a season: **W** (wins), **L** (losses), **SV** (saves), **G** (games pitched), **GS** (games started), **IP** (innings pitched), **H** (hits allowed) and **HR** (home runs allowed). Next we have two statistics that are rates: **BB/9** (walks per nine innings) and **K/9** (strikeouts per nine innings), before returning to the unadjusted K (strikeouts).

Next up is **GB%** (ground ball percentage), which is the percentage of all batted balls that were hit on the ground, including both outs and hits. Remember, this is based on observational data and subject to human error, so please approach this with a healthy dose of skepticism.

BABIP (batting average on balls in play) is calculated using the same methodology as it is for position players, but it often tells us more about a pitcher than it does a hitter. With pitchers, a high BABIP is often due to poor defense or bad luck, and can often be an indicator of potential rebound, and a low BABIP may be cause to expect performance regression. (A typical league-average BABIP is close to .290-.300.)

The metrics **WHIP** (walks plus hits per inning pitched) and **ERA** (earned run average) are old standbys: WHIP measures walks and hits allowed on a per-inning basis, while ERA measures earned runs on a nine-inning basis. Neither of these stats are translated or adjusted.

DRA- (Deserved Run Average) was described at length earlier, and measures how the pitcher "deserved" to perform compared to other pitchers. Please note that since we lack all the data points that would make for a "real" DRA for minor-league events, the DRA- displayed for minor league partial-seasons is based off of different data. (That data is a modified version of our cFIP metric, which you can find more information about on our website.)

Shane Bieber   RHP

Born: 05/31/95   Age: 26   Bats: R   Throws: R
Height: 6'3"   Weight: 200   Origin: Round 4, 2016 Draft (#122 overall)

YEAR	TEAM	LVL	AGE	W	L	SV	G	GS	IP	H	HR	BB/9	K/9	K	GB%	BABIP
2018	AKR	AA	23	3	0	0	5	5	31	26	1	0.3	8.7	30	47.3%	.278
2018	COL	AAA	23	3	1	0	8	8	48²	30	3	1.1	8.7	47	52.0%	.227
2018	CLE	MLB	23	11	5	0	20	19	114²	130	13	1.8	9.3	118	46.2%	.356
2019	CLE	MLB	24	15	8	0	34	33	214¹	186	31	1.7	10.9	259	44.4%	.298
2020	CLE	MLB	25	8	1	0	12	12	77¹	46	7	2.4	14.2	122	48.4%	.267
2021 FS	CLE	MLB	26	10	6	0	26	26	150	121	18	2.1	11.7	195	45.5%	.297
2021 DC	CLE	MLB	26	14	7	0	30	30	196.7	159	24	2.1	11.7	257	45.5%	.297

Comparables: Luis Severino, Danny Salazar, Joe Musgrove

YEAR	TEAM	LVL	AGE	WHIP	ERA	DRA-	WARP	MPH	FB%	WHF	CSP
2018	AKR	AA	23	0.87	1.16	61	0.9				
2018	COL	AAA	23	0.74	1.66	69	1.2				
2018	CLE	MLB	23	1.33	4.55	74	2.6	94.7	57.4%	26.2%	
2019	CLE	MLB	24	1.05	3.28	75	4.9	94.4	45.8%	30.8%	
2020	CLE	MLB	25	0.87	1.63	53	2.6	95.3	53.6%	40.7%	
2021 FS	CLE	MLB	26	1.04	2.44	64	4.4	94.7	50.0%	33.2%	44.2%
2021 DC	CLE	MLB	26	1.04	2.44	64	5.8	94.7	50.0%	33.2%	44.2%

Just like with hitters, **WARP** (Wins Above Replacement Player) is a total value metric that puts pitchers of all stripes on the same scale as position players. We use DRA as the primary input for our calculation of WARP. You might notice that relief pitchers (due to their limited innings) may have a lower WARP than you were expecting or than you might see in other WARP-like metrics. WARP does not take leverage into account, just the actions a pitcher performs and the expected value of those actions ... which ends up judging high-leverage relief pitchers differently than you might imagine given their prestige and market value.

MPH gives you the pitcher's 95th percentile velocity for the noted season, in order to give you an idea of what the *peak* fastball velocity a pitcher possesses. Since this comes from our pitch-tracking data, it is not publicly available for minor-league pitchers.

Finally, we display the three new pitching metrics we described earlier. **FB%** (fastball percentage) gives you the percentage of fastballs thrown out of all pitches. **WHF** (whiff rate) tells you the percentage of swinging strikes induced out of all pitches. **CSP** (called strike probability) expresses the likelihood of all pitches thrown to result in a called strike, after controlling for factors like handedness, umpire, pitch type, count and location.

PECOTA

All players have PECOTA projections for 2021, as well as a set of other numbers that describe the performance of comparable players according to PECOTA. All projections for 2021 are for the player at the date we went to press in early January and are projected into the league and park context as indicated by the team abbreviation. (Note that players at very low levels of the minors are too unpredictable to assess using these numbers.) All PECOTA projected statistics represent a player's projected major-league performance.

How we're doing that is a little different this season. There are really two different values that go into the final stat line that you see for PECOTA: How a player performs, and how much playing time he'll be given to perform it. In the past we've estimated playing time based on each team's roster and depth charts, and we'll continue to do that. These projections are denoted as **2021 DC**.

But in many cases, a player won't be projected for major-league playing time; most of the time this is because they aren't projected to be major-league players at all, but still developing as prospects. Or perhaps a player will provide Triple-A depth, only to have an opportunity open up because of injury. For these purposes, we're also supplying a second projection, labeled **2021 FS**, or full season. This is what we would project the player to provide in 600 plate appearances or 150 innings pitched.

Below the projections are the player's three highest-scoring comparable players as determined by PECOTA. All comparables represent a snapshot of how the listed player was performing at the same age as the current player, so if a

23-year-old pitcher is compared to Bartolo Colón, he's actually being compared to a 23-year-old Colón, not the version that pitched for the Rangers in 2018, nor to Colón's career as a whole.

A few points about pitcher projections. First, we aren't yet projecting peak velocity, so that column will be blank in the PECOTA lines. Second, projecting DRA is trickier than evaluating past performance, because it is unclear how deserving each pitcher will be of his anticipated outcomes. However, we know that another DRA-related statistic–contextual FIP or cFIP-estimates future run scoring very well. So for PECOTA, the projected DRA- figures you see are based on the past cFIPs generated by the pitcher and comparable players over time, along with the other factors described above.

If you're familiar with PECOTA, then you'll have noticed that the projection system often appears bullish on players coming off a bad year and bearish on players coming off a good year. (This is because the system weights several previous seasons, not just the most recent one.) In addition, we publish the 50th percentile projections for each player–which is smack in the middle of the range of projected production—which tends to mean PECOTA stat lines don't often have extreme results like 40 home runs or 250 strikeouts in a given season. In essence, PECOTA doesn't project very many extreme seasons.

Managers

After all those wonderful team chapters, we've got statistics for each big-league manager, all of whom are organized by alphabetical order. Here you'll find a block including an extraordinary amount of information collected from each manager's entire career. For more information on the acronyms and what they mean, please visit the Glossary at www.baseballprospectus.com.

There is one important metric that we'd like to call attention to, and you'll find it next to each manager's name: **wRM+** (weighted reliever management plus). Developed by Rob Arthur and Rian Watt, wRM+ investigates how good a manager is at using their best relievers during the moments of highest leverage, using both our proprietary DRA metric as well as Leverage Index. wRM+ is scaled to a league average of 100, and a wRM+ of 105 indicates that relievers were used approximately five percent "better" than average. On the other hand, a wRM+ of 95 would tell us the team used its relievers five percent "worse" than the average team.

While wRM+ does not have an extremely strong correlation with a manager, it is statistically significant; this means that a manager is not *entirely* responsible for a team's wRM+, but does have some effect on that number.

Part 1: Team Analysis

Performance Graphs

Payroll History (in millions)

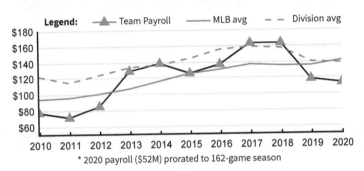

* 2020 payroll ($52M) prorated to 162-game season

Future Commitments (in millions)

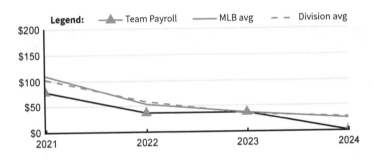

Farm System Ranking

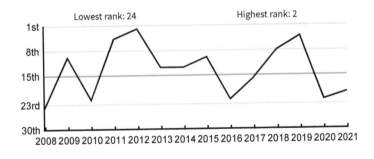

2020 Team Performance

ACTUAL STANDINGS

Team	W	L	Pct
TB	40	20	0.667
NYY	33	27	0.550
TOR	**32**	**28**	**0.533**
BAL	25	35	0.417
BOS	24	36	0.400

dWIN% STANDINGS

Team	W	L	Pct
NYY	33	27	0.560
TB	29	31	0.495
BOS	25	35	0.429
TOR	**25**	**35**	**0.425**
BAL	25	35	0.420

TOP HITTERS

Player	WARP
Lourdes Gurriel Jr.	1.7
Cavan Biggio	1.2
Teoscar Hernández	1.1

TOP PITCHERS

Player	WARP
Hyun Jin Ryu	1.5
Rafael Dolis	0.5
Taijuan Walker	0.5

VITAL STATISTICS

Statistic Name	Value	Rank
Pythagenpat	.484	17th
dWin%	.425	22nd
Runs Scored per Game	5.03	7th
Runs Allowed per Game	5.20	25th
Deserved Runs Created Plus	104	8th
Deserved Run Average Minus	116	28th
Fielding Independent Pitching	5.05	26th
Defensive Efficiency Rating	.689	24th
Batter Age	26.3	1st
Pitcher Age	29.8	26th
Payroll	$52.0M	19th
Marginal $ per Marginal Win	$2.5M	11th

2021 Team Projections

PROJECTED STANDINGS

Team	W	L	Pct	+/-
NYY	99.5	62.5	0.614	10
The starting rotation was loaded with risk even before Corey Kluber and Jameson Taillon became members. At least D.J. LeMahieu should keep the lineup humming.				
TB	86.0	76.0	0.531	-22
The defending AL champions didn't really spend their winter defending anything.				
TOR	**84.4**	**77.6**	**0.521**	**-2**
They stopped a starting pitcher short of credibly claiming favorite status, but adding George Springer gives them one of the junior circuit's most lethal lineups.				
BOS	79.3	82.7	0.490	14
There's a faint flavor of their 2012-13 offseason to what Boston did this winter, and look how that year turned out.				
BAL	66.1	95.9	0.408	-1
Mike Elias was forthright about his disinterest in winning in the short term. His winter proved he was serious.				

TOP PROJECTED HITTERS

Player	WARP
George Springer	5.3
Vladimir Guerrero Jr.	2.9
Danny Jansen	2.6

TOP PROJECTED PITCHERS

Player	WARP
Hyun Jin Ryu	3.4
Ross Stripling	1.8
Steven Matz	1.6

FARM SYSTEM REPORT

Top Prospect	Number of Top 101 Prospects
Austin Martin, #22	4

KEY DEDUCTIONS

Player	WARP
Anthony Bass	0.8
Jonathan Villar	0.8
Chase Anderson	0.4

KEY ADDITIONS

Player	WARP
George Springer	5.3
Marcus Semien	2.3
Steven Matz	1.6
Kirby Yates	1.2

Team Personnel

President & CEO
Mark A. Shapiro

Executive Vice President, Baseball Operations & General Manager
Ross Atkins

Senior Vice President, Player Personnel
Tony Lacava

Vice President, International Scouting
Andrew Tinnish

Assistant General Manager
Joe Sheehan

Manager
Charlie Montoyo

BP Alumni
Matt Bishoff

Rogers Centre Stats

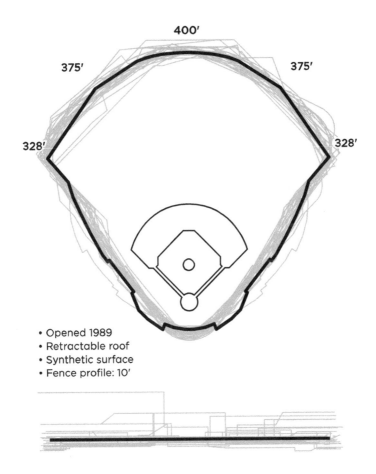

400'

375'   375'

328'   328'

- Opened 1989
- Retractable roof
- Synthetic surface
- Fence profile: 10'

Three-Year Park Factors

Runs	Runs/RH	Runs/LH	HR/RH	HR/LH
99	100	99	107	104

Blue Jays Team Analysis

The word "unprecedented" was ubiquitous in 2020. At times, it was tiresome to see that word annexed by corporations to serve as a preface to every advertisement, and yet it was a constant reminder of how far we had strayed from the normal we knew. But it is a fitting way to describe what happened August 26, when the members of the Milwaukee Bucks were scheduled to start their playoff game against the Orlando Magic. Instead, they refused to take the court.

The players were demanding justice and accountability for Jacob Blake, a 29-year-Black man who was shot in the back seven times by police in Kenosha, Wisconsin, about 40 miles from Milwaukee. The shooting fanned flames of anger that had been burning for weeks. Months. Years.

The team's collective action had an immediate impact. It made headlines and caught the attention of people outside and inside the sports world, including baseball players. Soon after, the Cincinnati Reds and Milwaukee Brewers announced their game was off too. The Dodgers-Giants and Mariners-Padres contests followed suit. Some Black players on other teams decided to sit out and let their teams play without them. That night's Red Sox-Blue Jays game was played as scheduled, the Bucks' protest coming too late for many teams in the eastern time zone to figure out how to react.

With more teams joining in the protest over the course of the next day, the Blue Jays held a team meeting to decide what to do. There were no African-Americans on the Jays roster that day; Anthony Alford, who had three hits in 16 at-bats (.188) for the season and struggled to find his footing with the team, had been designated for assignment the week before. There are a few Afro-Latino players on the Blue Jays, including Vladimir Guerrero Jr., Teoscar Hernández and Rafael Dolis. Being Afro-Latino comes with views on and experiences with blackness that can be similar to those of African-Americans, but can also be pretty distinct, so it's unclear what their relationship might be to the Black Lives Matter Movement and how they might have been feeling that day.

What we know is that the Blue Jays voted to play the game. Red Sox outfielder Jackie Bradley Jr., the only African-American on that team, told his teammates he didn't want to play that night and that he would be sitting out in protest. His decision led to a discussion among his colleagues, and the Red Sox decided to join him. It was only when informed of the Red Sox's decision not to play that the Blue Jays agreed to postpone. At a time when the ground felt like it was shifting in the world of men's professional sports, the Blue Jays chose to stand still.

⚾   ⚾   ⚾

After struggling for a few years in the post-Jose Bautista era, the prospect development team had done their work, and coming into last year, Blue Jays looked like a predictable team. The window was set to open; 2020 would be the first full year that the young stars of the future—Vladimir Guerrero Jr., Bo Bichette, Cavan Biggio, Teoscar Hernández—would play together. The organization did exactly what rising young teams are supposed to do, signing an ace for their rotation in Hyun-jin Ryu, who had been coming off a second-place finish in National League Cy Young Award voting. Maybe they weren't ready to challenge the AL East elite yet, but everything was going according to plan.

The Blue Jays, like many other Grapefruit League teams, were on the field, playing in two split-squad games when Rob Manfred first announced it was shutting down spring training and postponing the start of the season due to the coronavirus pandemic. Dreams of how the season would play out turned to questions of whether it would happen at all, as the league and its players fought bitterly and publicly about how baseball was to be played in 2020, and for how much. And while they were hashing out the details, George Floyd was murdered.

Many have theorized as to why his death, caused by a police officer who knelt on his neck for eight minutes and 46 seconds, became the catalyst that it did. It may have been the brutality of it, the fact it was caught on video, pandemic-induced solitude, a mix of the three or more. What's clear is that it took his death for many people to clue into the violence Black people face and have been facing for centuries. Cities across America boiled over in frustration, pain, and anger.

It was a movement not even Major League Baseball, a league that has never been known for activism, could ignore. Players started to speak out. It took nine days for the league to issue a statement—a statement that didn't include the words Black Lives Matter. "MLB is committed to engaging our communities to invoke change," the statement included, mentioning no specific changes or any indication of what that engagement would entail. The league was on it, probably.

In June, after weeks of negotiations, Major League Baseball finally imposed a 60-game season. As Opening Day approached, the Blue Jays scrambled to find a place to play home games after the Canadian government said "no thanks" to the idea of teams flying in and out of Toronto on a regular basis in a pandemic. They wound up playing at Sahlen Field in Buffalo, the home of the Blue Jays' Triple-A affiliate.

In 2017, Bruce Maxwell knelt during the national anthem, following the lead of NFL quarterback Colin Kaepernick, who sought to protest the unequal treatment of Black people and people of color in the U.S. At the time, the majority of fans equated the protest with disrespect for the nation's armed forces, and Maxwell's act drew heavy criticism. Prior to the 2020 season, he was the only major-league player to kneel. At the time, the majority of fans at the time equated the protest with disrespect of the nation's armed forces. But Floyd's death changed the conversation around kneeling throughout sports.

The public address announcer hadn't even finished announcing the name of the anthem singer when a handful of Blue Jays players—outfielder Anthony Alford, newly converted first baseman Guerrero Jr., shortstop Santiago Espinal and infielder Cavan Biggio—got down on one knee.

No one booed. No one cheered. There was no one to do so, since fans were officially barred due to the coronavirus. The anthem was a recording of Marvin Gaye's performance from the 1983 NBA All-Star Game, and crowd noise from the video made it sound, at least on TV, like the stadium wasn't as empty as it was. Some players wore masks or face coverings, and others didn't; some players stood a little farther apart, but not by much. Some of the Rays knelt as well. For more than two minutes, as Gaye crooned, the players, coaches and managers quietly contemplated the start of a new season, one that would be unlike any other.

A 600-foot black cloth lay on the ground as the anthem played. The cloth was supposed to symbolize unity—the idea came from veteran African-American outfielder Andrew McCutchen—and everyone on the field had been holding it before the anthem started. But both the cloth and the kneeling were league-sanctioned acts of protest. Kneeling when it's rubber-stamped by the league is one thing. Kneeling when Maxwell did, when you don't know if your teammates, let alone your team or the league, will have your back, is something else.

When asked what inspired him to kneel, Biggio, who is white, told reporters he took a knee to support Alford, who was hesitant to kneel due to the fact that he wasn't an everyday player. Alford told reporters he would have knelt regardless but appreciated the support. The action was stripped of its defiance, rendered almost sterile by the league's approval, and yet there was still a player who was worried about the repercussions.

⚾   ⚾   ⚾

The Jays got a taste of the scheduling havoc wrought by the virus pretty early on—a week into the season, a three-game set against the Phillies was postponed after the latter team revealed two staff members tested positive. The plans started to go awry, as they always do. On the field, the team was dealt a huge blow when closer Ken Giles hurt his elbow and landed on the injured list on opening weekend, effectively wiping out his season.

There were defensive miscues, a slow start by Ryu, an injury to rising star Bo Bichette and some frustratingly close games that all seemed to end in losses. They were the kind of gaffes that could easily be predicted out of a young team, and yet people, in their excitement, rarely do. But there were also bright spots: Teoscar Hernández started hitting and for a (short) time, led the league in home runs. Nate Pearson made his highly anticipated major-league debut. Lourdes Gurriel Jr. showed off in left field, making catches and notching assists as if he'd been an outfielder forever, and hadn't moved there after a cringeworthy case of the yips in 2019.

By August 27, the Blue Jays were a game above .500. The Blue Jays players were idle that day, after agreeing to postpone their game against the Red Sox. But general manager Ross Atkins, trying to bolster a depleted starting rotation, traded for Taijuan Walker.

Walker came to the Jays from the Seattle Mariners, where he was one of 10 African-American players. The Mariners voted not to play August 26, and Walker told reporters in his introductory news conference that it didn't feel right to play that day, and that he would have voiced that opinion if he had been with the Jays, too.

With Walker pitching well, Ryu starting to pick things up too and the bullpen sorting itself out, for the most part, thanks to guys like Anthony Kay, Jordan Romano, Rafael Dolis, AJ Cole and Julian Merryweather, the Jays did indeed eek their way into the playoffs with a 32-28 record, thanks to the expanded playoff format. After the lean years that followed the 2015 and 2016 seasons, it was pleasant and bizarre to watch them celebrate on an empty field in Buffalo, and eavesdrop from our couches on catcher Caleb Joseph delivering a rousing speech to his teammates.

They crashed and burned in the best two-of-three wild card series against the Rays, their season ending where it began, but vowed they would be back in the postseason soon enough. There's no reason to predict otherwise.

⚾   ⚾   ⚾

In many ways, the 2020 season was a triumph for the Blue Jays. No one got COVID-19, first and foremost. They made the playoffs ahead of schedule. The team improved and showed character in a lot of ways. But growth isn't only measured by what happens on the field.

Alford grew up in Mississippi; when he was 12 years old, a police officer drew a gun while searching the car he was in as he returned from a cottage with some friends. Like many Black people in the U.S., Canada, and elsewhere, he used his own experiences to explain the impact of anti-Black racism to the people around him. On Opening Day, Blue Jays infielder Rowdy Tellez, who is Jewish and Mexican, didn't kneel for the anthem, but put his hand on Alford's shoulder and talked about the impact of hearing Alford talk about his experiences. Both Biggio and Guerrero cited Alford's stories as a factor in their decision to kneel. Alford and Bichette also had conversations about race and its impact on opportunity.

In the aftermath of George Floyd's death, Black people around the world shared those kinds of stories more than ever, no doubt hoping that adding their voice to the chorus would help underscore that racism isn't a concept, it is a real thing that real people deal with on a regular basis.

Sitting out for one baseball game, a game they knew would be postponed, seemed like a relatively low-stakes way to signal support for that change. But on August 27, when the Blue Jays had to make a choice, instead of taking a stand, they took the field. In Alford's absence, did anyone step up to give a rousing speech and remind their teammates of the stories they'd heard him tell? If Alford or Walker had been in the room, would that have changed things, transformed an abstract concept into something personal, tangible? If their teammates had been forced to look two Black men in the eye while voting to play, would it have made a difference?

If someone had tried to tell me at the beginning of 2020 that the actions of players in the WNBA and NBA to highlight anti-Black racism would even move the needle in baseball, I would have laughed out loud. What took place was an unquestionable step forward. But for the Blue Jays, after two months of protests and anger and sadness and people baring their souls, there weren't enough people in the room that day who wanted to do a small thing, but a large gesture, to show their support for basic human rights. Where does that leave us?

Some progress is better than none, of course. But wearing a t-shirt is easy. Holding a black cloth during the national anthem is easy. Committing yourself to engaging communities to invoke change is easy, at least easy to say. Creating lasting change is not. The Blue Jays didn't step up when they had the chance. Maybe more than anything else, the team's reticence is a lesson for its fans and a reflection of its burgeoning on-field talent: Things are starting to change, but there's still a ways left to go. ▪

—Kamila Hinkson is a journalist for CBC Montreal.

Part 2: Player Analysis

PLAYER COMMENTS WITH GRAPHS

Bo Bichette SS
Born: 03/05/98   Age: 23   Bats: R   Throws: R
Height: 6'0"   Weight: 185   Origin: Round 2, 2016 Draft (#66 overall)

YEAR	TEAM	LVL	AGE	PA	R	2B	3B	HR	RBI	BB	K	SB	CS	AVG/OBP/SLG
2018	NH	AA	20	595	95	43	7	11	74	48	101	32	11	.286/.343/.453
2019	BUF	AAA	21	244	34	16	2	8	32	19	48	15	5	.275/.333/.473
2019	TOR	MLB	21	212	32	18	0	11	21	14	50	4	4	.311/.358/.571
2020	TOR	MLB	22	128	18	9	1	5	23	5	27	4	1	.301/.328/.512
2021 FS	TOR	MLB	23	600	86	31	2	21	76	39	140	13	6	.264/.318/.448
2021 DC	TOR	MLB	23	617	88	32	2	22	79	40	144	13	6	.264/.318/.448

Comparables: Willy Adames, Alex Rodriguez, Gleyber Torres

Before three innings had been played between the Jays and the Marlins on August 12, the Jays found themselves down 8-0. Bichette was the second batter up in the bottom of the third. He singled with one out, starting a rally that brought in two runs.

It was the beginning of an astonishing comeback, a seven-homer onslaught from the Jays' young bats, and at the center of it all, Bichette was electrifying. He had five hits in six plate appearances, one of them a homer; he stole two bases. The Marlins added three in the fifth, extending their lead even further. But the Jays kept coming, finally tying the game on back-to-back homers from Bichette and Shaw in the eighth. And then they lost—three runs from the Marlins in the top of the 10th. Bichette led off the bottom of the inning with a walk, but no one drove him in. In spite of everything, they sank to 6-9 on the season. A week later, Bichette was gone entirely, the victim of a knee sprain that left him out of the lineup for a month.

Bichette was, at the time of the injury, the Jays' best hitter. More than that, he was an emotional cornerstone of the team, always at the center of everything, always the face the camera focused on when it cut to the dugout. The Jays, before his injury, seemed to be losing in spite of him; when, after he was gone, they won seven in a row and vaulted themselves into postseason contention, they were winning in spite of his absence. He played in fewer than half of their games, but he finished the year as their fourth-best position player. He is still only 22 years old. And when you think of these young Jays, he continues to be the person you think of: rounding the bases after a double, hair flying, or leaping to greet a teammate after a home run, or staring out after a loss, all the expectations of a sparkling future heavy in his face.

YEAR	TEAM	LVL	AGE	PA	DRC+	BABIP	BRR	FRAA	WARP
2018	NH	AA	20	595	124	.331	3.2	SS(116): -4.0, 2B(9): 0.6	3.1
2019	BUF	AAA	21	244	102	.317	-2.0	SS(51): -1.4, 2B(1): -0.0	0.8
2019	TOR	MLB	21	212	109	.368	-0.8	SS(42): 4.6	1.5
2020	TOR	MLB	22	128	111	.352	-0.9	SS(26): 0.9	0.3
2021 FS	TOR	MLB	23	600	105	.319	0.8	SS 0, 2B 0	2.3
2021 DC	TOR	MLB	23	617	105	.319	0.8	SS 0	2.4

Bo Bichette, continued

Batted Ball Distribution

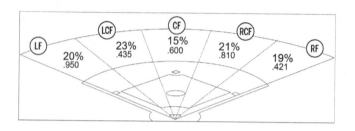

Strike Zone vs LHP   *Strike Zone vs RHP*

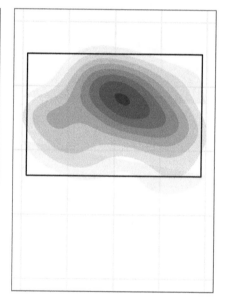

Cavan Biggio 2B

Born: 04/11/95   Age: 26   Bats: L   Throws: R
Height: 6'2"   Weight: 200   Origin: Round 5, 2016 Draft (#162 overall)

YEAR	TEAM	LVL	AGE	PA	R	2B	3B	HR	RBI	BB	K	SB	CS	AVG/OBP/SLG
2018	NH	AA	23	563	80	23	5	26	99	100	148	20	8	.252/.388/.499
2019	BUF	AAA	24	174	23	8	1	6	27	34	28	5	1	.312/.448/.514
2019	TOR	MLB	24	430	66	17	2	16	48	71	123	14	0	.234/.364/.429
2020	TOR	MLB	25	265	41	16	0	8	28	41	61	6	0	.250/.375/.432
2021 FS	TOR	MLB	26	600	83	23	2	20	70	90	157	9	3	.232/.355/.410
2021 DC	TOR	MLB	26	606	84	23	2	21	71	90	159	9	3	.232/.355/.410

Comparables: Yoán Moncada, Rickie Weeks Jr., Ryan McMahon

Biggio provides hope for the smallest kid on every Little League team: You too can be great. All you have to do is not swing. The patron saint of patience posted the third-lowest swing percentage among qualified major-league hitters, and finished first at refusing to chase, even bettering one Mike Trout. Beyond the walks, Biggio enjoyed the advantages inherent in going 1-0 more often than he went 0-1, employing his limited power to turn fastball counts into line drives over the infielders. The question is whether this unique profile will hold up: He doesn't actually post the phenomenal contact rates you usually see from those who live by singles and walks, and pitchers have yet to challenge him with strikes and try to punish his reticence. Until they do, Biggio's on-base skills and inherited knack for positional versatility—he also acquitted himself well at third—put him among the Jays' best position players, and he adds an interesting dimension to a lineup full of big swings and barrels.

YEAR	TEAM	LVL	AGE	PA	DRC+	BABIP	BRR	FRAA	WARP
2018	NH	AA	23	563	135	.307	3.6	2B(68): 1.5, 3B(34): -1.1, 1B(22): 0.7	3.5
2019	BUF	AAA	24	174	149	.352	0.5	2B(22): 2.0, 1B(7): 0.2, 3B(7): 0.2	1.7
2019	TOR	MLB	24	430	112	.309	2.2	2B(85): 0.5, 1B(8): -0.7, RF(8): -0.9	2.1
2020	TOR	MLB	25	265	116	.311	0.5	2B(37): -0.3, RF(14): -0.5, 3B(10): 0.1	1.2
2021 FS	TOR	MLB	26	600	109	.296	0.0	3B -1, 2B 0	2.2
2021 DC	TOR	MLB	26	606	109	.296	0.0	3B -1, 2B 0	2.0

Cavan Biggio, continued

Batted Ball Distribution

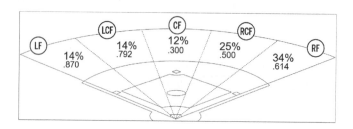

Strike Zone vs LHP   Strike Zone vs RHP

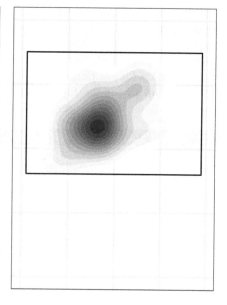

Santiago Espinal 2B

Born: 11/13/94   Age: 26   Bats: R   Throws: R
Height: 5'10"   Weight: 181   Origin: Round 10, 2016 Draft (#298 overall)

YEAR	TEAM	LVL	AGE	PA	R	2B	3B	HR	RBI	BB	K	SB	CS	AVG/OBP/SLG
2018	DUN	HI-A	23	73	9	3	1	2	8	6	10	0	3	.262/.333/.431
2018	SAL	HI-A	23	281	53	15	3	7	32	18	35	9	1	.312/.363/.477
2018	NH	AA	23	164	17	9	2	1	20	14	22	2	1	.286/.354/.395
2019	NH	AA	24	409	46	21	1	5	57	35	50	10	11	.278/.343/.381
2019	BUF	AAA	24	112	11	6	0	2	14	7	23	2	2	.317/.360/.433
2020	TOR	MLB	25	66	10	4	0	0	6	4	16	1	0	.267/.308/.333
2021 FS	TOR	MLB	26	600	71	27	1	12	63	42	130	6	3	.243/.302/.368
2021 DC	TOR	MLB	26	92	10	4	0	1	9	6	20	0	1	.243/.302/.368

Comparables: Pablo Reyes, Brock Holt, Josh Rojas

While he showed little aptitude for hitting over his time with the Jays, especially not for any kind of power, Espinal's solid fielding was enough to keep him on the infield through the injury to Bo Bichette. He even got two innings on the mound in one of the Jays' many blowouts. And he was of critical assistance to Vlad Jr. when he needed someone to get his celebration GoPro on. An all-around useful player, indeed.

YEAR	TEAM	LVL	AGE	PA	DRC+	BABIP	BRR	FRAA	WARP
2018	DUN	HI-A	23	73	106	.283	-0.7	SS(8): 0.7, 2B(6): 0.3, 3B(2): -0.3	0.2
2018	SAL	HI-A	23	281	151	.336	5.2	SS(53): 2.0, 3B(4): -0.3, 2B(2): 0.1	2.8
2018	NH	AA	23	164	108	.328	1.3	2B(16): 0.4, 3B(12): -0.1, SS(12): -1.0	0.5
2019	NH	AA	24	409	125	.310	-2.5	2B(52): 3.3, SS(22): 0.9, CF(12): 3.3	3.0
2019	BUF	AAA	24	112	100	.392	0.9	2B(18): 1.9, SS(11): -0.1	0.6
2020	TOR	MLB	25	66	86	.356	0.1	SS(21): 3.6, 3B(2): -0.0, P(2): -0.0	0.4
2021 FS	TOR	MLB	26	600	82	.298	-0.3	SS 1, 2B 1	0.5
2021 DC	TOR	MLB	26	92	82	.298	0.0	SS 0, 2B 0	0.1

Santiago Espinal, continued

Batted Ball Distribution

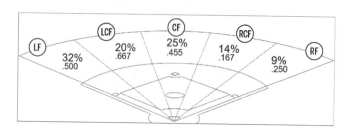

Strike Zone vs LHP   Strike Zone vs RHP

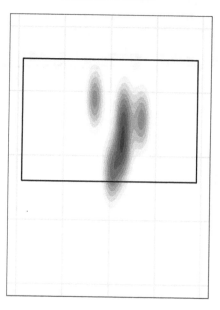

Type	Frequency	Velocity	H Movement	V Movement
● Fastball	100.0%	70.6 [30]	-7.9 [94]	-40.4 [29]

Randal Grichuk CF

Born: 08/13/91   Age: 29   Bats: R   Throws: R
Height: 6'2"   Weight: 216   Origin: Round 1, 2009 Draft (#24 overall)

YEAR	TEAM	LVL	AGE	PA	R	2B	3B	HR	RBI	BB	K	SB	CS	AVG/OBP/SLG
2018	TOR	MLB	26	462	60	32	1	25	61	27	122	3	2	.245/.301/.502
2019	TOR	MLB	27	628	75	29	5	31	80	35	163	2	1	.232/.280/.457
2020	TOR	MLB	28	231	38	9	0	12	35	13	49	1	1	.273/.312/.481
2021 FS	TOR	MLB	29	600	78	28	2	29	89	38	160	5	2	.239/.295/.457
2021 DC	TOR	MLB	29	509	66	24	1	24	75	32	135	4	2	.239/.295/.457

Comparables: Preston Wilson, Rick Ankiel, Colby Rasmus

For a moment there, it seemed like we might have been witnessing the birth of a new, powerful, fully-realized Grichuk: Over a few weeks in August, he was unstoppable. Then, of course, he stopped, and it became clear that this is what Grichuk has always done. He is the definition of a streaky player, who will have, every so often, hot stretches so hot that they make you believe, followed by long periods of nothingness. But on a team for whom defense has been an ongoing area of concern, Grichuk is still a stabilizing element in the outfield. His catch at the wall to save the clinching game against the Yankees on September 24, at least, endeared him to Jays fans for a few days. (Until he struck out five times in two games in the Wild Card series.)

YEAR	TEAM	LVL	AGE	PA	DRC+	BABIP	BRR	FRAA	WARP
2018	TOR	MLB	26	462	109	.282	2.5	RF(102): 2.4, CF(26): -2.3, LF(1): -0.0	1.9
2019	TOR	MLB	27	628	90	.266	-0.2	RF(92): -3.2, CF(62): -4.9	0.1
2020	TOR	MLB	28	231	101	.299	1.0	CF(48): -2.4	0.5
2021 FS	TOR	MLB	29	600	99	.283	-0.2	LF 0, CF -1	1.3
2021 DC	TOR	MLB	29	509	99	.283	-0.1	LF 0, CF -1	1.1

Randal Grichuk, continued

Batted Ball Distribution

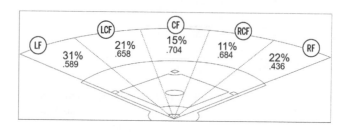

Strike Zone vs LHP   ### Strike Zone vs RHP

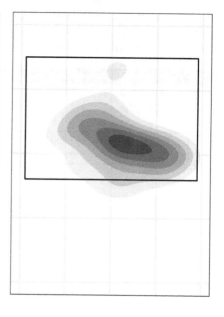

Vladimir Guerrero Jr. 3B

Born: 03/16/99 Age: 22 Bats: R Throws: R
Height: 6'2" Weight: 250 Origin: International Free Agent, 2015

YEAR	TEAM	LVL	AGE	PA	R	2B	3B	HR	RBI	BB	K	SB	CS	AVG/OBP/SLG
2018	NH	AA	19	266	48	19	1	14	60	21	27	3	3	.402/.449/.671
2018	BUF	AAA	19	128	15	7	0	6	16	15	10	0	0	.336/.414/.564
2019	BUF	AAA	20	34	7	1	0	3	8	4	2	1	0	.367/.441/.700
2019	TOR	MLB	20	514	52	26	2	15	69	46	91	0	1	.272/.339/.433
2020	TOR	MLB	21	243	34	13	2	9	33	20	38	1	0	.262/.329/.462
2021 FS	TOR	MLB	22	600	79	32	1	22	84	52	103	3	2	.278/.347/.466
2021 DC	TOR	MLB	22	607	80	32	1	22	85	53	104	3	2	.278/.347/.466

Comparables: Adrián Beltré, Ryan Zimmerman, Eric Chavez

There was little more frustrating to the spirit of the long-suffering Jays fan than watching an early-2020 Vlad plate appearance, the outcome of which always seemed to be the same: a ball absolutely scorched—just demolished—straight into the ground. Guerrero struggled to elevate throughout his rookie campaign, with an average launch angle of just over six degrees. But that total was nothing compared to the early weeks of the 2020 season. In August, though his hard-hit rate on fastballs was over 55 percent, his average launch angle on those pitches was one degree. One degree! When he hit the ball in the air, there was a good chance that you would see it leave the yard—but why couldn't it be hit in the air more often? Combine the frustrated expectations with the growing pains of someone playing a position for the first time without the benefit of a full spring training to adjust, and there was a lot to wring one's hands over.

And yet, as was the case the year prior, Guerrero was still an above-average hitter. He not only maintained his low strikeout rate, but lowered it. And in September, particularly during the season's final weeks, there was a dazzling glimpse of the player that was promised, the player that very well still could be. On September 17, Guerrero struck out on a Masahiro Tanaka slider. Nine games passed until he struck out again. He batted .342/.375/.632 over the 11 games from September 18 to the regular season's end. His average launch angle on fastballs over that time, and for the entire month of September, jumped all the way up to 13.

Since the Jays' early postseason exit, Guerrero has expressed a renewed commitment to focus on conditioning and training. Though it's been said in every assessment of his somewhat underwhelming big-league performance so far, it's worth repeating because it's true: He's still only 21 years old. If these early seasons are just the growing pains, then they've been pretty exceptional.

Toronto Blue Jays 2021

YEAR	TEAM	LVL	AGE	PA	DRC+	BABIP	BRR	FRAA	WARP
2018	NH	AA	19	266	192	.402	-2.9	3B(53): 1.0	2.9
2018	BUF	AAA	19	128	185	.323	-4.8	3B(25): 4.3	1.4
2019	BUF	AAA	20	34	158	.320	-0.2	3B(7): 0.1	0.3
2019	TOR	MLB	20	514	100	.308	-3.5	3B(96): -5.1	0.9
2020	TOR	MLB	21	243	106	.282	0.4	1B(34): 1.9	0.8
2021 FS	TOR	MLB	22	600	121	.309	-0.6	1B 3, 3B 0	3.0
2021 DC	TOR	MLB	22	607	121	.309	-0.6	1B 3, 3B 0	2.9

Vladimir Guerrero Jr., continued

Batted Ball Distribution

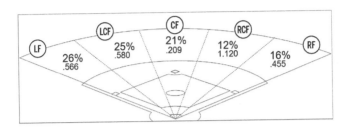

Strike Zone vs LHP   ### *Strike Zone vs RHP*

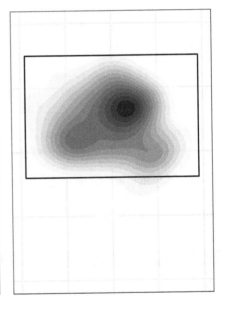

Lourdes Gurriel Jr. LF

Born: 10/10/93   Age: 27   Bats: R   Throws: R
Height: 6'4"   Weight: 215   Origin: International Free Agent, 2016

YEAR	TEAM	LVL	AGE	PA	R	2B	3B	HR	RBI	BB	K	SB	CS	AVG/OBP/SLG
2018	NH	AA	24	65	7	3	1	2	14	3	8	1	1	.322/.354/.508
2018	BUF	AAA	24	156	20	8	0	5	30	4	34	3	2	.293/.321/.449
2018	TOR	MLB	24	263	30	8	0	11	35	9	59	1	2	.281/.309/.446
2019	BUF	AAA	25	130	18	13	0	4	26	3	23	0	2	.276/.308/.480
2019	TOR	MLB	25	343	52	19	2	20	50	20	86	6	4	.277/.327/.541
2020	TOR	MLB	26	224	28	14	0	11	33	14	48	3	1	.308/.348/.534
2021 FS	TOR	MLB	27	600	78	30	1	25	88	30	142	4	3	.263/.309/.460
2021 DC	TOR	MLB	27	565	74	28	1	24	83	28	134	3	3	.263/.309/.460

Comparables: Geoff Jenkins, Alfonso Soriano, Trey Mancini

Gurriel's signing to a seven-year deal in late 2016 was one of the first, defining moves of the Shapiro/Atkins regime—a major international signing, full of potential, with the second son of one of Cuba's premier baseball families coming to Toronto. Four years down the line, that potential only seems more exciting. Gurriel hit the ground running in his rookie season, but with each successive year, he shores up the weaknesses in his game and adds more dazzle to the parts that already had shine. His approach at the plate, with its often wild swings and misses, became more focused; he swung at better pitches, whiffed less often and forced pitchers to throw him strikes. When he hit the ball, as he often did, he hit it with authority. He benefitted, too, from a second season as a permanent outfielder, showing off a powerful arm to lead the league in putouts.

Best of all, he managed to avoid injury. His two major-league seasons before this were nearly as truncated, in terms of games played, as the 2020 season. But those were on account of being hurt: ankles, knees, an errant appendix. This year, he played in all but three games, only seeming to get stronger as the season went on; he nearly hit for the cycle in the final game of the season. Gurriel, along with his outfield-mate Hernandez, has been a delight to watch both on the field and in the dugout.

YEAR	TEAM	LVL	AGE	PA	DRC+	BABIP	BRR	FRAA	WARP
2018	NH	AA	24	65	129	.333	0.3	2B(7): -0.1, SS(5): -0.7	0.3
2018	BUF	AAA	24	156	116	.345	-0.9	SS(23): 0.9, 2B(9): 0.2, 1B(1): 0.2	0.7
2018	TOR	MLB	24	263	104	.326	-1.7	SS(46): -0.8, 2B(24): -1.1	0.8
2019	BUF	AAA	25	130	104	.309	-3.6	2B(12): -1.1, SS(7): -2.0, LF(7): -1.0	-0.2
2019	TOR	MLB	25	343	112	.318	2.0	LF(63): -0.1, 2B(9): -1.3, 1B(3): -0.3	1.5
2020	TOR	MLB	26	224	112	.351	0.4	LF(53): 8.2, 1B(1): -0.0	1.7
2021 FS	TOR	MLB	27	600	107	.311	-0.5	LF 3, 1B 0	2.5
2021 DC	TOR	MLB	27	565	107	.311	-0.4	LF 3	2.1

Lourdes Gurriel Jr., continued

Batted Ball Distribution

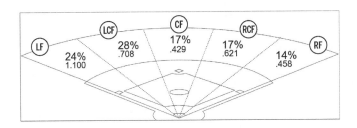

Strike Zone vs LHP   ## Strike Zone vs RHP

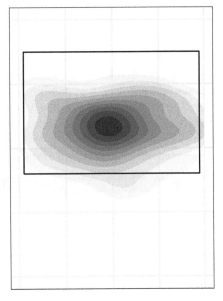

Teoscar Hernández LF

Born: 10/15/92   Age: 28   Bats: R   Throws: R
Height: 6'2"   Weight: 205   Origin: International Free Agent, 2011

YEAR	TEAM	LVL	AGE	PA	R	2B	3B	HR	RBI	BB	K	SB	CS	AVG/OBP/SLG
2018	TOR	MLB	25	523	67	29	7	22	57	41	163	5	5	.239/.302/.468
2019	BUF	AAA	26	83	11	0	1	5	11	6	21	3	0	.253/.313/.480
2019	TOR	MLB	26	464	58	19	2	26	65	45	153	6	3	.230/.306/.472
2020	TOR	MLB	27	207	33	7	0	16	34	14	63	6	1	.289/.340/.579
2021 FS	TOR	MLB	28	600	84	26	2	33	92	49	191	11	5	.242/.311/.482
2021 DC	TOR	MLB	28	528	74	23	2	29	81	43	168	9	5	.242/.311/.482

Comparables: Pete Incaviglia, Bo Jackson, Geoff Jenkins

The power has always been there with Hernández; that much is clear. There have been so many tantalizing several-week stretches over the course of his time with the Jays that have hinted at what might be lurking: not just an above-average hitter, as he's been throughout his career so far, but someone beyond even that. Those hot streaks, though, have so often been followed by frigid ones. That began to change in the second half of 2019, and in the two-plus months that constituted the 2020 season, Hernández blossomed. He hit the ball harder than ever before, he cut his (still sky-high) strikeout rate, and, more than anything else, he didn't ever stop hitting. A great first week in July gave way to a scorching August, wherein Hernández alone seemed like he could have generated enough energy to power the team indefinitely. And though an oblique injury slowed his September, his final month, taken as a whole, still fueled optimism. And unlikely as it might have seemed when they acquired him from the Astros in 2017, Hernández, too, has become one of the faces of this team, vibrant and ever-smiling — one of the most important contributors to their success this season, and a vital part of the core group moving forward.

YEAR	TEAM	LVL	AGE	PA	DRC+	BABIP	BRR	FRAA	WARP
2018	TOR	MLB	25	523	103	.313	-0.1	LF(87): -2.0, RF(35): 0.7	1.3
2019	BUF	AAA	26	83	84	.280	0.8	CF(9): -1.5, LF(5): 0.3	0.0
2019	TOR	MLB	26	464	100	.293	-0.4	CF(79): -0.8, LF(46): 9.6	2.4
2020	TOR	MLB	27	207	123	.348	-1.1	RF(40): -2.6, CF(9): -0.2	1.1
2021 FS	TOR	MLB	28	600	111	.309	0.6	RF 3, LF 0	2.8
2021 DC	TOR	MLB	28	528	111	.309	0.5	RF 3	2.2

Teoscar Hernández, continued

Batted Ball Distribution

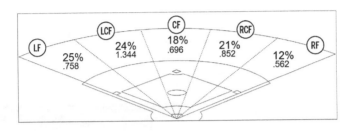

Strike Zone vs LHP   ## *Strike Zone vs RHP*

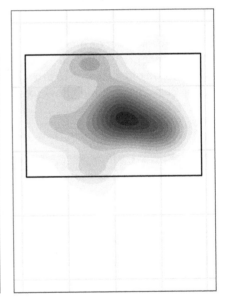

Danny Jansen   C

Born: 04/15/95   Age: 26   Bats: R   Throws: R
Height: 6'2"   Weight: 225   Origin: Round 16, 2013 Draft (#475 overall)

YEAR	TEAM	LVL	AGE	PA	R	2B	3B	HR	RBI	BB	K	SB	CS	AVG/OBP/SLG
2018	BUF	AAA	23	360	45	21	1	12	58	44	49	5	1	.275/.390/.473
2018	TOR	MLB	23	95	12	6	0	3	8	9	17	0	0	.247/.347/.432
2019	TOR	MLB	24	384	41	12	1	13	43	31	79	0	1	.207/.279/.360
2020	TOR	MLB	25	147	18	3	0	6	20	21	31	0	0	.183/.312/.358
2021 FS	TOR	MLB	26	600	81	25	1	21	73	64	126	1	1	.238/.335/.412
2021 DC	TOR	MLB	26	343	46	14	0	12	41	37	72	0	1	.238/.335/.412

Comparables: Ryan Doumit, Charles Johnson, Mickey Tettleton

Canadian Zunino took all the things that helped him take a step forward in 2019 and did them a little more. Jansen can't match his division rival's muscle at the plate (his exit velocity ranks near the bottom among even catchers), but he sticks to his approach anyway, which is to swing at pitches he can homer on and let the

YEAR	TEAM	P. COUNT	FRM RUNS	BLK RUNS	THRW RUNS	TOT RUNS
2018	TOR	3610	0.6	0.7	-0.2	1.1
2018	BUF	7752	-4.6	0.2	-0.1	-4.8
2019	TOR	14805	10.9	2.1	0.4	13.4
2020	TOR	6284	0.1	0.8	0.0	0.9
2021	TOR	13228	5.5	3.6	0.3	9.5
2021	TOR	13228	5.5	3.2	0.3	9.0

rest go. It's not pretty baseball—even Mario Mendoza posted a .250 BABIP—but it does the job often enough to provide value. Add to that his excellent defense, and the Blue Jays shouldn't have to worry about their catching position for the rest of this contention cycle.

YEAR	TEAM	LVL	AGE	PA	DRC+	BABIP	BRR	FRAA	WARP
2018	BUF	AAA	23	360	137	.292	0.2	C(56): -6.0	1.7
2018	TOR	MLB	23	95	100	.274	0.9	C(29): 1.0	0.7
2019	TOR	MLB	24	384	82	.230	-0.7	C(103): 11.9	2.2
2020	TOR	MLB	25	147	108	.190	-1.0	C(43): 0.2	0.7
2021 FS	TOR	MLB	26	600	107	.276	-0.9	C 12	4.2
2021 DC	TOR	MLB	26	343	107	.276	-0.5	C 9	2.6

Danny Jansen, continued

Batted Ball Distribution

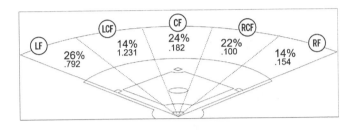

Strike Zone vs LHP   ## Strike Zone vs RHP

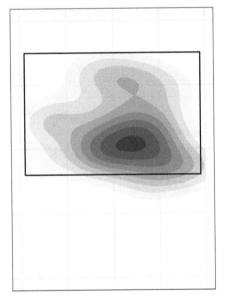

Joe Panik 2B

Born: 10/30/90   Age: 30   Bats: L   Throws: R
Height: 6'1"   Weight: 205   Origin: Round 1, 2011 Draft (#29 overall)

YEAR	TEAM	LVL	AGE	PA	R	2B	3B	HR	RBI	BB	K	SB	CS	AVG/OBP/SLG
2018	SF	MLB	27	392	38	14	1	4	24	26	30	4	2	.254/.307/.332
2019	SF	MLB	28	388	33	17	1	3	27	36	38	4	2	.235/.310/.317
2019	NYM	MLB	28	103	17	4	1	2	12	7	9	0	0	.277/.333/.404
2020	TOR	MLB	29	141	18	6	0	1	7	20	27	0	0	.225/.340/.300
2021 FS	TOR	MLB	30	600	60	26	2	12	60	59	86	5	2	.245/.327/.372

Comparables: Mark Loretta, Frank Bolling, Gene Baker

Now entering his 30s, Panik did not blossom into a slugger in 2020. He did not even return to being a league-average hitter. An extremely slow start at the plate, fueled in part by an uncharacteristic tendency to swing and miss, had Jays fans weeping and gnashing their teeth. But improvements at the plate toward the end of the season—and a fantastic walk rate—netted him more consistent playing time, and saved countless dental visits before year's end.

YEAR	TEAM	LVL	AGE	PA	DRC+	BABIP	BRR	FRAA	WARP
2018	SF	MLB	27	392	86	.265	1.0	2B(94): 4.3, 1B(1): 0.1	1.1
2019	SF	MLB	28	388	86	.254	-0.5	2B(90): 5.0	1.0
2019	NYM	MLB	28	103	91	.289	-0.1	2B(28): -1.4	0.1
2020	TOR	MLB	29	141	94	.283	0.6	2B(18): -2.7, SS(14): 1.1, 3B(12): -1.4	0.0
2021 FS	TOR	MLB	30	600	93	.272	-0.3	2B 0, SS 1	1.2

Joe Panik, continued

Batted Ball Distribution

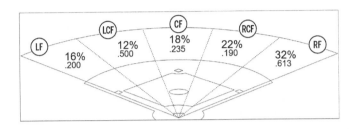

Strike Zone vs LHP   ## Strike Zone vs RHP

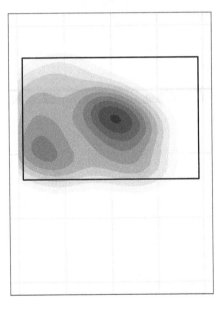

Marcus Semien SS

Born: 09/17/90   Age: 30   Bats: R   Throws: R
Height: 6'0"   Weight: 195   Origin: Round 6, 2011 Draft (#201 overall)

YEAR	TEAM	LVL	AGE	PA	R	2B	3B	HR	RBI	BB	K	SB	CS	AVG/OBP/SLG
2018	OAK	MLB	27	703	89	35	2	15	70	61	131	14	6	.255/.318/.388
2019	OAK	MLB	28	747	123	43	7	33	92	87	102	10	8	.285/.369/.522
2020	OAK	MLB	29	236	28	9	1	7	23	25	50	4	0	.223/.305/.374
2021 FS	TOR	MLB	30	600	86	26	2	23	77	59	133	9	5	.246/.323/.432
2021 DC	TOR	MLB	30	612	88	26	2	23	79	60	136	10	5	.246/.323/.432

Comparables: Woodie Held, Jhonny Peralta, Khalil Greene

It's rare to have a star position player for whom excellence in hitting is a secondary quality, but for a fleeting few seasons the A's had two such players in Ramón Laureano and Semien. In the latter case, that's dependent on agreement with FRAA's stellar evaluation as opposed to some conflicting metrics, but suffice it to say Semien is an especially well-rounded player when that trait is becoming something of a given league-wide. Semien's walk year was a step back from a 2019 that saw him as the best hitter on the A's, amounting to a WARP among the 10 best in the majors. A reversion to the league-average hitting of past seasons left it unclear if Oakland declining to tender a qualifying offer was typical A's stinginess or characteristic of a cold reception looming on the open market.

YEAR	TEAM	LVL	AGE	PA	DRC+	BABIP	BRR	FRAA	WARP
2018	OAK	MLB	27	703	98	.296	5.4	SS(159): 16.2	5.4
2019	OAK	MLB	28	747	134	.294	1.8	SS(161): 4.2	7.5
2020	OAK	MLB	29	236	101	.260	1.4	SS(53): 7.4	1.6
2021 FS	TOR	MLB	30	600	105	.286	0.3	SS 0	2.3
2021 DC	TOR	MLB	30	612	105	.286	0.3	2B 0, SS 0	2.3

Marcus Semien, continued

Batted Ball Distribution

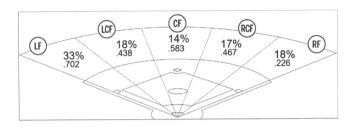

Strike Zone vs LHP   Strike Zone vs RHP

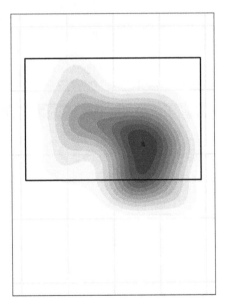

Travis Shaw 3B

Born: 04/16/90   Age: 31   Bats: L   Throws: R
Height: 6'4"   Weight: 230   Origin: Round 9, 2011 Draft (#292 overall)

YEAR	TEAM	LVL	AGE	PA	R	2B	3B	HR	RBI	BB	K	SB	CS	AVG/OBP/SLG
2018	MIL	MLB	28	587	73	23	0	32	86	78	108	5	2	.241/.345/.480
2019	SA	AAA	29	174	27	4	0	12	33	36	37	3	1	.286/.437/.586
2019	MIL	MLB	29	270	22	5	0	7	16	36	89	0	0	.157/.281/.270
2020	TOR	MLB	30	180	17	10	0	6	17	16	50	0	0	.239/.306/.411
2021 FS	TOR	MLB	31	600	72	24	1	26	79	64	165	4	2	.223/.314/.423
2021 DC	TOR	MLB	31	375	45	15	0	16	49	40	103	3	1	.223/.314/.423

Comparables: Dean Palmer, Wilson Betemit, Phil Nevin

After a disastrous 2019 at the plate, Shaw's 2020 was something of a bounce-back, though it wasn't exactly a great showing. His strikeout rate fell, but remained sky-high, as did his whiff rate; he also walked at a lower rate than he has in four years. He was clearly hitting the ball hard, but it didn't seem to translate into much results-wise. The Blue Jays are left with what will be a common question: Were 60 games just not enough for the exit velocity to find its way into the slugging percentage? Or had it already, hidden by the greater regression of Being Travis Shaw? What he did have to offer was a competent third base, which, in the wake of Vlad Jr.'s move to first, was something the Jays needed. Though no longer: Given the organization's surfeit of minor-league reinforcements, they chose to non-tender Shaw in the autumn.

YEAR	TEAM	LVL	AGE	PA	DRC+	BABIP	BRR	FRAA	WARP
2018	MIL	MLB	28	587	120	.242	-0.7	3B(107): 1.8, 2B(39): -0.5, 1B(17): 0.0	3.5
2019	SA	AAA	29	174	160	.299	-2.1	3B(23): 1.0, 1B(10): 0.4, 2B(2): -0.1	1.6
2019	MIL	MLB	29	270	70	.216	0.1	3B(71): 2.3, 1B(6): 0.2, 2B(2): -0.0	0.2
2020	TOR	MLB	30	180	94	.306	-1.3	3B(37): 1.6, 1B(14): 1.1	0.4
2021 FS	TOR	MLB	31	600	96	.272	-0.5	3B 2, 2B 0	1.0
2021 DC	TOR	MLB	31	375	96	.272	-0.3	3B 1, 2B 0	0.6

Travis Shaw, continued

Batted Ball Distribution

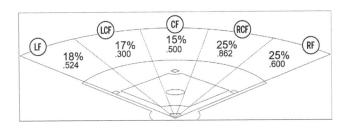

Strike Zone vs LHP   Strike Zone vs RHP

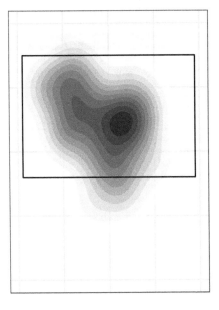

George Springer   OF

Born: 09/19/89   Age: 31   Bats: R   Throws: R
Height: 6'3"   Weight: 221   Origin: Round 1, 2011 Draft (#11 overall)

YEAR	TEAM	LVL	AGE	PA	R	2B	3B	HR	RBI	BB	K	SB	CS	AVG/OBP/SLG
2018	HOU	MLB	28	620	102	26	0	22	71	64	122	6	4	.265/.346/.434
2019	HOU	MLB	29	556	96	20	3	39	96	67	113	6	2	.292/.383/.591
2020	HOU	MLB	30	222	37	6	2	14	32	24	38	1	2	.265/.359/.540
2021 FS	TOR	MLB	31	600	106	26	1	33	81	69	129	6	5	.273/.369/.522
2021 DC	TOR	MLB	31	634	112	27	1	35	86	73	137	7	5	.273/.369/.522

Comparables: Jay Buhner, Danny Tartabull, Reggie Jackson

Springer was born less than two hours from Gillette Stadium and grew up a Patriots fan. He appears to have learned something from his boyhood team about responding to accusations of cheating: he resumed his consistent excellence without missing a beat. Where other Astros seemed deflated offensively by the scandal, Springer proved that spying on opponents is entirely unnecessary for him to dominate. He followed up regular season career bests in strikeout rate and DRC+ by maintaining a postseason record that's so successful it might as well have been orchestrated by Bill Belichick.

YEAR	TEAM	LVL	AGE	PA	DRC+	BABIP	BRR	FRAA	WARP
2018	HOU	MLB	28	620	114	.303	1.5	CF(80): -2.8, RF(77): 2.6, LF(1): -0.0	2.9
2019	HOU	MLB	29	556	140	.305	2.5	CF(75): 2.4, RF(59): 4.1	5.4
2020	HOU	MLB	30	222	141	.259	0.0	CF(42): -2.0, RF(9): -1.5	1.3
2021 FS	TOR	MLB	31	600	140	.304	-0.2	CF 0, LF 0	4.8
2021 DC	TOR	MLB	31	634	140	.304	-0.2	CF 0	5.3

George Springer, continued

Batted Ball Distribution

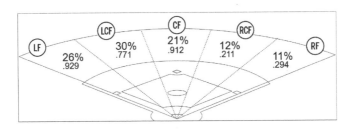

Strike Zone vs LHP   *Strike Zone vs RHP*

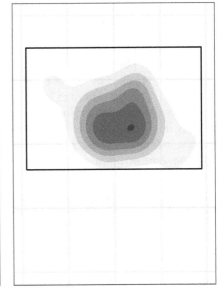

Rowdy Tellez   1B

Born: 03/16/95   Age: 26   Bats: L   Throws: L
Height: 6'4"   Weight: 255   Origin: Round 30, 2013 Draft (#895 overall)

YEAR	TEAM	LVL	AGE	PA	R	2B	3B	HR	RBI	BB	K	SB	CS	AVG/OBP/SLG
2018	BUF	AAA	23	444	43	22	0	13	50	40	74	7	4	.270/.340/.425
2018	TOR	MLB	23	73	10	9	0	4	14	2	21	0	0	.314/.329/.614
2019	BUF	AAA	24	109	20	9	0	7	21	14	25	0	0	.366/.450/.688
2019	TOR	MLB	24	409	49	19	0	21	54	29	116	1	1	.227/.293/.449
2020	TOR	MLB	25	127	20	5	0	8	23	11	20	0	1	.283/.346/.540
2021 FS	TOR	MLB	26	600	81	26	1	29	88	54	138	0	1	.249/.325/.464
2021 DC	TOR	MLB	26	528	71	22	0	26	78	48	121	0	1	.249/.325/.464

Comparables: Fernando Seguignol, Tony Clark, Mike Jacobs

After the disappointment of 2019, Tellez thrived in his newfound platoon role in 2020. He started slow, gathered steam through August, then absolutely exploded in September, batting .387/.444/.613 through the nine games he played. Tragically for both Tellez and the Jays, a knee injury knocked him out for the rest of the regular season, though he did make a surprise appearance in the Jays' brief postseason stint, recording a hit and eventually coming around to score in his lone at-bat.

Tellez is a fan favorite, a 30th-round pick who worked his way through the system before a breakout in Triple-A, a survivor of hardship on and off the field. The questions raised by last year's struggles about his long-term viability as a player were especially hard to hear about someone whose journey has been one of the team's most profound stories. All the more satisfying, then, to see his success, even in this shortened season: the mashing of lefties, the vast improvement in his two-strike approach and the attendant drop in his strikeout rate, the same power that he flashed in his 2018 September callup. Tellez has played himself into the Jays' future, at least the not-too-distant one.

YEAR	TEAM	LVL	AGE	PA	DRC+	BABIP	BRR	FRAA	WARP
2018	BUF	AAA	23	444	122	.298	-0.8	1B(107): -3.0	0.6
2018	TOR	MLB	23	73	101	.391	-0.1	1B(17): -0.4	0.1
2019	BUF	AAA	24	109	175	.435	-1.6	1B(26): 1.9	1.1
2019	TOR	MLB	24	409	91	.267	-1.1	1B(57): 4.3	0.5
2020	TOR	MLB	25	127	118	.276	0.1	1B(19): -0.9	0.3
2021 FS	TOR	MLB	26	600	108	.284	-1.0	1B 0	1.4
2021 DC	TOR	MLB	26	528	108	.284	-0.9	1B 0	1.3

Rowdy Tellez, continued

Batted Ball Distribution

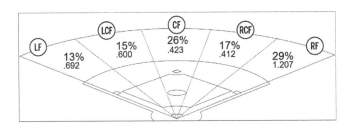

Strike Zone vs LHP   Strike Zone vs RHP

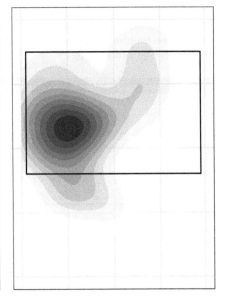

Ryan Borucki   LHP

Born: 03/31/94   Age: 27   Bats: L   Throws: L
Height: 6'4"   Weight: 215   Origin: Round 15, 2012 Draft (#475 overall)

YEAR	TEAM	LVL	AGE	W	L	SV	G	GS	IP	H	HR	BB/9	K/9	K	GB%	BABIP
2018	BUF	AAA	24	6	5	0	13	13	77	62	6	3.3	6.8	58	51.8%	.255
2018	TOR	MLB	24	4	6	0	17	17	97²	96	7	3.0	6.2	67	47.0%	.294
2019	BUF	AAA	25	1	0	0	2	2	11	11	4	2.5	7.4	9	42.4%	.241
2019	TOR	MLB	25	0	1	0	2	2	6²	15	2	8.1	8.1	6	39.3%	.500
2020	TOR	MLB	26	1	1	0	21	0	16²	12	1	6.5	11.3	21	35.0%	.282
2021 FS	TOR	MLB	27	2	2	0	57	0	50	48	7	3.8	8.9	49	43.3%	.296
2021 DC	TOR	MLB	27	2	2	0	57	0	48	46	7	3.8	8.9	47	43.3%	.296

Comparables: Anthony Banda, Walker Lockett, Daniel Norris

The good news is that Borucki managed to exceed his 2019 total of 6⅓ laborious innings. The better news is that he managed to stay healthy through the 2020 season. And the best news of all is that, in a bullpen role that looks to continue into next season, Borucki thrived. All but three of his 21 appearances were scoreless; all three of his pitches saw upticks in velocity; and increased usage of his new and improved slider-cutter proved incredibly effective, serving as his putaway pitch. He ended the season as one of the Jays' most trusted high-leverage relievers—pretty good for someone who didn't even make the Opening Day roster.

YEAR	TEAM	LVL	AGE	WHIP	ERA	DRA-	WARP	MPH	FB%	WHF	CSP
2018	BUF	AAA	24	1.17	3.27	84	1.2				
2018	TOR	MLB	24	1.32	3.87	101	0.9	93.3	58.7%	19.4%	
2019	BUF	AAA	25	1.27	4.91	105	0.2				
2019	TOR	MLB	25	3.15	10.80	180	-0.2	93.6	52.3%	23.7%	
2020	TOR	MLB	26	1.44	2.70	94	0.2	96.4	47.8%	32.6%	
2021 FS	TOR	MLB	27	1.39	4.39	101	0.2	94.4	54.3%	24.3%	45.9%
2021 DC	TOR	MLB	27	1.39	4.39	101	0.3	94.4	54.3%	24.3%	45.9%

Ryan Borucki, continued

Pitch Shape vs LHH

Pitch Shape vs RHH

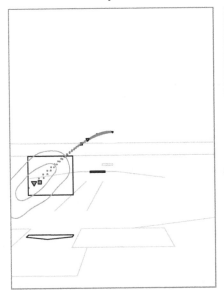
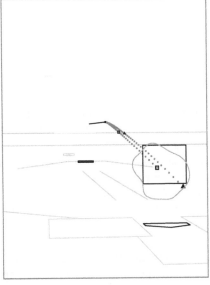

Type	Frequency	Velocity	H Movement	V Movement
□ Sinker	47.7%	94.9 [113]	15.2 [84]	-19 [105]
▲ Changeup	14.2%	85 [99]	12.3 [97]	-24 [110]
▽ Slider	37.8%	86.7 [112]	-2.9 [91]	-29.2 [113]

Tyler Chatwood   RHP

Born: 12/16/89   Age: 31   Bats: R   Throws: R
Height: 5'11"   Weight: 200   Origin: Round 2, 2008 Draft (#74 overall)

YEAR	TEAM	LVL	AGE	W	L	SV	G	GS	IP	H	HR	BB/9	K/9	K	GB%	BABIP
2018	IOW	AAA	28	0	1	0	2	2	6²	5	0	13.5	5.4	4	61.1%	.278
2018	CHC	MLB	28	4	6	0	24	20	103²	92	9	8.2	7.4	85	51.5%	.291
2019	CHC	MLB	29	5	3	2	38	5	76²	65	8	4.3	8.7	74	52.9%	.286
2020	CHC	MLB	30	2	2	0	5	5	18²	22	2	4.3	12.1	25	38.5%	.400
2021 FS	TOR	MLB	31	2	3	0	57	0	50	46	6	5.8	9.3	51	49.3%	.297
2021 DC	TOR	MLB	31	3	3	0	62	0	54	50	7	5.8	9.3	55	49.3%	.297

Comparables: Chris Tillman, Wily Peralta, Erasmo Ramírez

On July 1, 2020, Netflix released a rebooted version of *Unsolved Mysteries*, the popular documentary TV show that originally aired on NBC in the late-'80s. Among the phenomena investigated were ghosts in Japan, UFO sightings in Berkshire County, Mass. and a prison escape in Ohio. If the series gets another season, they should explore what would've happened if Chatwood had been able to play a full season in 2020. Much maligned after signing a three-year, $38 million deal with the Cubs ahead of the 2018 campaign, Chatwood went back to the rotation for the start of this season and struck out 19 and allowed just one earned run in his first 12 ⅔ innings. He got lit up in his third start, so maybe there isn't much intrigue, but a forearm strain limited him to only 3 ⅔ innings the rest of the way. The arsenal adjustments he made—decreased usage of the four-seamer, an improved cutter and more cutter usage—were enough to make you wonder if he has staying power in the rotation once again. Maybe we'll find out next season, either on Netflix or on the field.

YEAR	TEAM	LVL	AGE	WHIP	ERA	DRA-	WARP	MPH	FB%	WHF	CSP
2018	IOW	AAA	28	2.25	9.45	126	0.0				
2018	CHC	MLB	28	1.80	5.30	162	-2.4	95.1	58.9%	22.3%	
2019	CHC	MLB	29	1.33	3.76	79	1.3	97.7	71.0%	25.2%	
2020	CHC	MLB	30	1.66	5.30	88	0.3	96.2	51.7%	29.3%	
2021 FS	TOR	MLB	31	1.57	4.89	106	0.1	96.5	63.3%	24.9%	44.3%
2021 DC	TOR	MLB	31	1.57	4.89	106	0.2	96.5	63.3%	24.9%	44.3%

Tyler Chatwood, continued

Pitch Shape vs LHH

Pitch Shape vs RHH

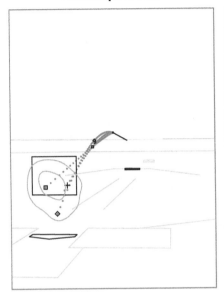
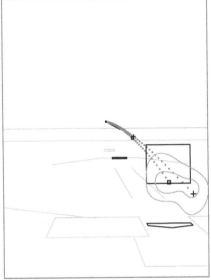

Type	Frequency	Velocity	H Movement	V Movement
● Fastball	7.9%	94.9 [107]	-2.9 [118]	-14.9 [101]
□ Sinker	43.8%	94.4 [110]	-12.1 [107]	-16.8 [112]
+ Cutter	29.9%	90.1 [111]	4.1 [115]	-26.4 [91]
▲ Changeup	5.1%	85.6 [102]	-9.6 [111]	-25.1 [106]
◇ Curveball	13.3%	80.5 [107]	8.7 [104]	-48.5 [100]

A.J. Cole   RHP

Born: 01/05/92   Age: 29   Bats: R   Throws: R
Height: 6'5"   Weight: 240   Origin: Round 4, 2010 Draft (#116 overall)

YEAR	TEAM	LVL	AGE	W	L	SV	G	GS	IP	H	HR	BB/9	K/9	K	GB%	BABIP
2018	WAS	MLB	26	1	1	0	4	2	10¹	16	6	5.2	8.7	10	21.6%	.345
2018	NYY	MLB	26	3	1	0	28	0	38	39	9	3.8	11.6	49	35.9%	.319
2019	COL	AAA	27	0	1	2	13	0	17	10	2	2.6	11.1	21	36.1%	.235
2019	CLE	MLB	27	3	1	1	25	0	26	31	4	2.8	10.4	30	30.0%	.360
2020	TOR	MLB	28	3	0	1	24	0	23¹	19	3	3.5	7.7	20	33.3%	.258
2021 FS	TOR	MLB	29	2	2	0	57	0	50	45	8	3.6	9.1	50	35.1%	.277

Comparables: Mike Foltynewicz, Jon Gray, Kevin Gausman

Cole outperformed his DRA by a significant margin. His slider generated far fewer whiffs than it has in recent seasons. His strikeout rate dropped. How, then, did he manage to be so successful? One could point to the addition of a cutter, or improved performance on his fastball that always seemed to barely avoid the sweet spot of the bat. Either way, he was an unexpectedly valuable contributor to the Jays' August bullpen success.

YEAR	TEAM	LVL	AGE	WHIP	ERA	DRA-	WARP	MPH	FB%	WHF	CSP
2018	WAS	MLB	26	2.13	13.06	174	-0.3	94.2	45.1%	18.3%	
2018	NYY	MLB	26	1.45	4.26	64	0.9	95.7	30.9%	36.8%	
2019	COL	AAA	27	0.88	3.18	56	0.6				
2019	CLE	MLB	27	1.50	3.81	132	-0.3	96.0	45.0%	30.3%	
2020	TOR	MLB	28	1.20	3.09	112	0.1	95.3	44.1%	27.3%	
2021 FS	TOR	MLB	29	1.30	4.11	95	0.4	95.6	41.4%	30.0%	45.6%

A.J. Cole, continued

Pitch Shape vs LHH

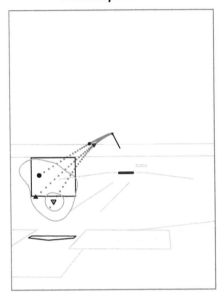

Pitch Shape vs RHH

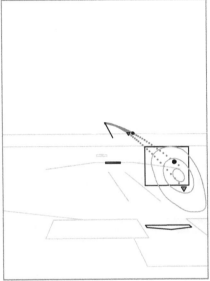

Type	Frequency	Velocity	H Movement	V Movement
● Fastball	33.9%	93.5 [103]	-7.4 [97]	-13 [106]
+ Cutter	9.3%	88.6 [102]	-1.8 [76]	-21 [113]
▲ Changeup	7.8%	86.4 [105]	-15.5 [80]	-25.3 [106]
▽ Slider	45.0%	83.6 [98]	1.6 [86]	-29.8 [111]

Rafael Dolis RHP

Born: 01/10/88   Age: 33   Bats: R   Throws: R
Height: 6'4"   Weight: 235   Origin: International Free Agent, 2004

YEAR	TEAM	LVL	AGE	W	L	SV	G	GS	IP	H	HR	BB/9	K/9	K	GB%	BABIP
2020	TOR	MLB	32	2	2	5	24	0	24	16	1	5.2	11.6	31	46.3%	.294
2021 FS	TOR	MLB	33	2	2	4	57	0	50	44	6	4.3	9.8	54	49.8%	.295
2021 DC	TOR	MLB	33	2	2	4	57	0	54	47	6	4.3	9.8	58	49.8%	.295

Comparables: Jeremy Jeffress, Ryan Brasier, Anthony Bass

What a long, strange trip it's been for Dolis, who prior to this season hadn't pitched in the majors since 2013. The Jays signed him from NPB's Hanshin Tigers in January, where his numbers were solid, but he was understandably something of an unknown quantity to most fans. As it turned out, Dolis proved a critical part of the Jays' unexpected bullpen success in 2020. Striking out 31 percent of the batters he faced, effectively limiting hard contact and working at a micro-nap-friendly deliberate pace, Dolis and his sinker-slider-splitter mix came second only to Hyun-Jin Ryu in terms of pitcher importance to the Jays. All the more delightful, then, that he came as such a surprise.

YEAR	TEAM	LVL	AGE	WHIP	ERA	DRA-	WARP	MPH	FB%	WHF	CSP
2020	TOR	MLB	32	1.25	1.50	76	0.5	96.2	61.1%	30.4%	
2021 FS	TOR	MLB	33	1.37	3.91	90	0.5	96.2	61.1%	30.4%	41.3%
2021 DC	TOR	MLB	33	1.37	3.91	90	0.5	96.2	61.1%	30.4%	41.3%

Rafael Dolis, continued

Pitch Shape vs LHH

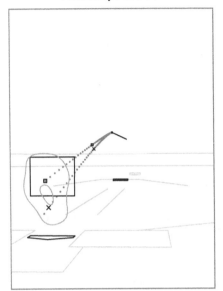

Pitch Shape vs RHH

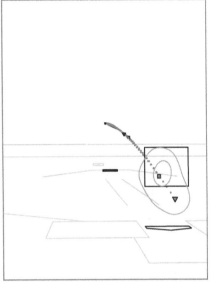

Type	Frequency	Velocity	H Movement	V Movement
● Fastball	5.3%	94.1 [105]	-12.7 [71]	-13.9 [104]
☐ Sinker	55.8%	94.8 [112]	-12.8 [102]	-15.1 [118]
✕ Splitter	18.6%	86.7 [107]	-8.6 [97]	-25.7 [112]
▽ Slider	20.3%	84 [100]	6 [103]	-36.6 [92]

Wilmer Font   RHP

Born: 05/24/90   Age: 31   Bats: R   Throws: R
Height: 6'4"   Weight: 255   Origin: International Free Agent, 2006

YEAR	TEAM	LVL	AGE	W	L	SV	G	GS	IP	H	HR	BB/9	K/9	K	GB%	BABIP
2018	TB	MLB	28	2	1	0	9	5	27	15	2	3.7	6.7	20	45.3%	.178
2018	LAD	MLB	28	0	2	0	6	0	10¹	18	5	0.9	6.1	7	42.5%	.371
2018	OAK	MLB	28	0	0	0	4	0	6²	13	5	5.4	12.2	9	33.3%	.421
2019	NYM	MLB	29	1	2	0	15	3	31	29	8	3.8	7.0	24	35.8%	.241
2019	TOR	MLB	29	2	3	0	23	14	39¹	34	7	2.5	12.1	53	35.1%	.300
2019	TB	MLB	29	1	0	0	10	0	14	15	2	3.2	11.6	18	43.2%	.371
2020	TOR	MLB	30	1	3	0	21	0	16¹	28	2	5.0	8.3	15	35.0%	.448
2021 FS	TOR	MLB	31	2	2	0	57	0	50	46	9	3.4	8.7	48	37.2%	.280

Comparables: Burch Smith, Matt Magill, Tyler Chatwood

Font was designated for assignment mere hours before the Jays clinched a playoff berth, which sums up how well this season went for him. Hints of competence were almost always followed by unmitigated disasters. Over Font's final three appearances for the Jays, he allowed five hits, five runs and five walks while recording just five outs; toward the end of the season, the mere announcement of his name, the sight of him jogging out of the bullpen, became enough to induce an overwhelming sense of despair. It was one of those seasons where absolutely nothing worked. The only comfort for Font is that it was a short one. He'll join the SK Wyverns, who have had no shortage of disappointment of late.

YEAR	TEAM	LVL	AGE	WHIP	ERA	DRA-	WARP	MPH	FB%	WHF	CSP
2018	TB	MLB	28	0.96	1.67	144	-0.4	97.5	63.6%	21.3%	
2018	LAD	MLB	28	1.84	11.32	157	-0.2	96.3	69.5%	16.1%	
2018	OAK	MLB	28	2.55	14.85	84	0.1	96.9	68.5%	29.7%	
2019	NYM	MLB	29	1.35	4.94	134	-0.4	96.9	58.5%	24.7%	
2019	TOR	MLB	29	1.14	3.66	73	0.8	96.8	61.8%	29.0%	
2019	TB	MLB	29	1.43	5.79	103	0.1	96.5	50.9%	29.6%	
2020	TOR	MLB	30	2.27	9.92	110	0.1	97.1	70.1%	19.3%	
2021 FS	TOR	MLB	31	1.31	4.32	99	0.3	96.9	62.4%	24.8%	47.4%

Wilmer Font, continued

Pitch Shape vs LHH

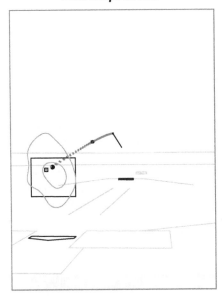

Pitch Shape vs RHH

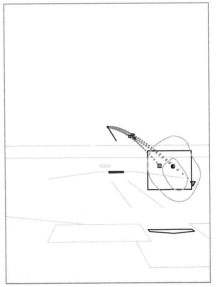

Type	Frequency	Velocity	H Movement	V Movement
● Fastball	51.9%	95.1 [108]	-5.6 [105]	-11.9 [109]
□ Sinker	18.2%	94.5 [111]	-11.3 [113]	-14.1 [121]
✕ Splitter	6.0%	84.9 [98]	-3.5 [116]	-29.7 [99]
▽ Slider	15.2%	86.1 [110]	3.7 [94]	-28.4 [116]
◇ Curveball	8.7%	76.6 [92]	9.3 [107]	-52.2 [91]

Thomas Hatch   RHP

Born: 09/29/94   Age: 26   Bats: R   Throws: R
Height: 6'1"   Weight: 205   Origin: Round 3, 2016 Draft (#104 overall)

YEAR	TEAM	LVL	AGE	W	L	SV	G	GS	IP	H	HR	BB/9	K/9	K	GB%	BABIP
2018	TNS	AA	23	8	6	0	26	26	143²	127	16	3.8	7.3	117	42.4%	.285
2019	NH	AA	24	2	3	0	6	6	35¹	25	5	0.5	8.7	34	50.0%	.241
2019	TNS	AA	24	4	10	0	21	21	100	104	13	3.3	8.4	93	35.5%	.329
2020	TOR	MLB	25	3	1	0	17	1	26¹	18	2	4.4	7.9	23	45.1%	.232
2021 FS	TOR	MLB	26	2	3	0	57	0	50	49	8	3.8	8.2	45	41.2%	.289
2021 DC	TOR	MLB	26	5	4	0	40	6	60.3	59	10	3.8	8.2	54	41.2%	.289

Comparables: Keury Mella, Chris Dwyer, Bobby Parnell

Despite his less-than-sparkling DRA, Hatch made an unexpectedly impressive showing in his rookie season, appearing in 17 games and leaving nothing but footprints in most of them. Thanks to being free from the shackles of the academy over the offseason—he finished up his degree in finance in the winter of 2018-19—Hatch had more time to ramp up his throwing program and monitor his health, avoiding the injuries that hampered his performance in 2019. His high-spin fastball, paired with a changeup and a whiff-inducing slider, made him a trusted option in almost any relief situation. If he keeps it up, he'll give himself more personal finances to manage once he hits arbitration.

YEAR	TEAM	LVL	AGE	WHIP	ERA	DRA-	WARP	MPH	FB%	WHF	CSP
2018	TNS	AA	23	1.31	3.82	94	1.5				
2019	NH	AA	24	0.76	2.80	76	0.5				
2019	TNS	AA	24	1.41	4.59	115	-0.8				
2020	TOR	MLB	25	1.18	2.73	105	0.2	96.6	57.4%	31.2%	
2021 FS	TOR	MLB	26	1.40	4.77	107	0.0	96.6	57.4%	31.2%	42.1%
2021 DC	TOR	MLB	26	1.40	4.77	107	0.1	96.6	57.4%	31.2%	42.1%

Thomas Hatch, continued

Pitch Shape vs LHH

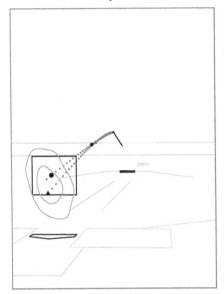

Pitch Shape vs RHH

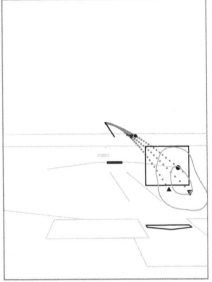

Type	Frequency	Velocity	H Movement	V Movement
● Fastball	47.4%	95.6 [110]	-6.6 [100]	-12.8 [107]
□ Sinker	6.6%	95.2 [114]	-13.6 [96]	-17.3 [110]
+ Cutter	3.4%	90.8 [115]	1.3 [96]	-21.1 [112]
▲ Changeup	25.2%	85.9 [103]	-6.9 [126]	-27.5 [100]
▽ Slider	17.5%	87.6 [116]	4.7 [98]	-27.9 [117]

Anthony Kay LHP

Born: 03/21/95   Age: 26   Bats: L   Throws: L
Height: 6'0"   Weight: 225   Origin: Round 1, 2016 Draft (#31 overall)

YEAR	TEAM	LVL	AGE	W	L	SV	G	GS	IP	H	HR	BB/9	K/9	K	GB%	BABIP
2018	COL	LO-A	23	4	4	0	13	13	69¹	73	6	2.9	10.1	78	43.3%	.358
2018	STL	HI-A	23	3	7	0	10	10	53¹	51	1	4.6	7.6	45	38.2%	.327
2019	BNG	AA	24	7	3	0	12	12	66¹	38	2	3.1	9.5	70	34.4%	.226
2019	BUF	AAA	24	2	2	0	7	7	36	33	3	5.5	9.8	39	39.6%	.323
2019	SYR	AAA	24	1	3	0	7	7	31¹	40	7	3.2	7.5	26	28.0%	.367
2019	TOR	MLB	24	1	0	0	3	2	14	15	0	3.2	8.4	13	54.5%	.341
2020	TOR	MLB	25	2	0	0	13	0	21	22	3	6.0	9.4	22	37.1%	.322
2021 FS	TOR	MLB	26	9	9	0	26	26	150	147	26	4.2	8.6	142	37.9%	.292
2021 DC	TOR	MLB	26	4	4	0	32	6	55	54	9	4.2	8.6	52	37.9%	.292

Comparables: Gregory Soto, Conner Menez, Alex Reyes

The Blue Jays enrolled Kay in the Earl Weaver Official Starter Certification program, working him into the major leagues by employing him in the middle innings of close games, bridging the gap to the setup men. The traits that qualified him for entry remain, and he still projects as a decent enough starter, but his 2020 performance did raise some concerns. Kay struggled to persuade batters to chase his pitches, especially his curve, which he tended to spike into the clay. This often put him behind in the count, and it often stayed that way. All this bears all the hallmarks of a slow Tommy John recovery; Kay's success will depend on tunneling the fastball and the curve better to put batters on their heels, and reclaiming the initiative.

YEAR	TEAM	LVL	AGE	WHIP	ERA	DRA-	WARP	MPH	FB%	WHF	CSP
2018	COL	LO-A	23	1.37	4.54	85	1.0				
2018	STL	HI-A	23	1.46	3.88	87	0.7				
2019	BNG	AA	24	0.92	1.49	54	1.9				
2019	BUF	AAA	24	1.53	2.50	127	0.2				
2019	SYR	AAA	24	1.63	6.61	120	0.3				
2019	TOR	MLB	24	1.43	5.79	97	0.1	95.1	61.6%	24.2%	
2020	TOR	MLB	25	1.71	5.14	112	0.0	96.1	56.5%	26.1%	
2021 FS	TOR	MLB	26	1.45	4.88	109	0.7	95.8	58.0%	25.6%	46.2%
2021 DC	TOR	MLB	26	1.45	4.88	109	0.1	95.8	58.0%	25.6%	46.2%

Anthony Kay, continued

Pitch Shape vs LHH

Pitch Shape vs RHH

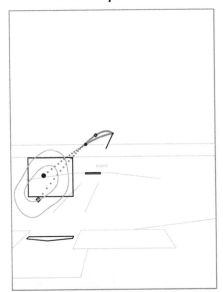
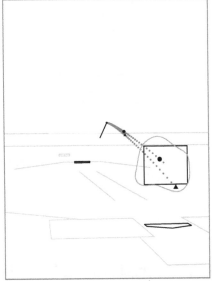

Type		Frequency	Velocity	H Movement	V Movement
●	Fastball	55.9%	93.8 [104]	5.8 [104]	-14.1 [103]
▲	Changeup	17.9%	86.4 [105]	9.8 [110]	-24 [110]
◇	Curveball	23.0%	78 [98]	-9.3 [107]	-50.2 [96]

Walker Lockett RHP

Born: 05/03/94   Age: 27   Bats: R   Throws: R
Height: 6'5"   Weight: 225   Origin: Round 4, 2012 Draft (#135 overall)

YEAR	TEAM	LVL	AGE	W	L	SV	G	GS	IP	H	HR	BB/9	K/9	K	GB%	BABIP
2018	ELP	AAA	24	5	9	0	23	23	133¹	145	17	2.2	8.0	118	45.8%	.327
2018	SD	MLB	24	0	3	0	4	3	15	22	4	6.0	7.2	12	55.6%	.360
2019	STL	HI-A	25	1	0	0	2	2	7	8	1	0.0	7.7	6	52.2%	.318
2019	SYR	AAA	25	3	3	0	11	10	59	75	5	1.7	5.9	39	54.5%	.343
2019	NYM	MLB	25	1	1	0	9	4	22²	33	6	2.4	6.4	16	41.2%	.370
2020	TOR	MLB	26	1	0	0	7	1	16¹	21	2	2.2	6.1	11	42.9%	.352
2021 FS	TOR	MLB	27	2	3	0	57	0	50	54	8	2.4	6.6	36	47.2%	.299

Comparables: Drew Anderson, John Gant, Lucas Sims

When you're a sinkerballer with a 41.8 percent groundball rate, you tend to move around a lot. Lockett shuffled the deck in 2020, favoring his good curveball and abandoning his four-seamer for the aforementioned sinker, but he struggled to get it down in the zone, so it was really just a less-fast fastball. The Mariners claimed him off waivers in September, the Blue Jays in December, and the Doosan Bears of the KBO shortly after. He'll have one last chance to reinvent himself; the real tragedy is that there are only so many pitches one can learn.

YEAR	TEAM	LVL	AGE	WHIP	ERA	DRA-	WARP	MPH	FB%	WHF	CSP
2018	ELP	AAA	24	1.33	4.72	86	2.3				
2018	SD	MLB	24	2.13	9.60	135	-0.1	94.3	55.5%	21.4%	
2019	STL	HI-A	25	1.14	5.14	85	0.1				
2019	SYR	AAA	25	1.46	3.66	91	1.3				
2019	NYM	MLB	25	1.72	8.34	101	0.2	94.4	54.3%	16.0%	
2020	TOR	MLB	26	1.53	4.96	102	0.1	95.0	34.8%	20.7%	
2021 FS	TOR	MLB	27	1.35	4.55	105	0.1	94.6	46.7%	18.8%	51.5%

Walker Lockett, continued

Pitch Shape vs LHH

Pitch Shape vs RHH

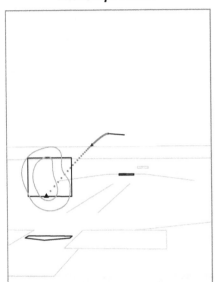
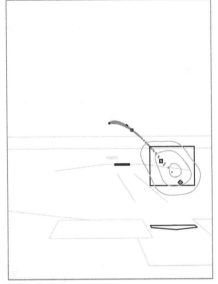

Type	Frequency	Velocity	H Movement	V Movement
☐ Sinker	34.3%	93.5 [105]	-12.4 [105]	-21.6 [96]
+ Cutter	20.9%	90.3 [112]	1.9 [100]	-22.8 [105]
▲ Changeup	22.2%	87.2 [108]	-12.8 [94]	-28.2 [98]
◇ Curveball	22.2%	80.9 [109]	7.7 [101]	-43.1 [112]

Steven Matz LHP

Born: 05/29/91   Age: 30   Bats: R   Throws: L
Height: 6'2"   Weight: 201   Origin: Round 2, 2009 Draft (#72 overall)

YEAR	TEAM	LVL	AGE	W	L	SV	G	GS	IP	H	HR	BB/9	K/9	K	GB%	BABIP
2018	NYM	MLB	27	5	11	0	30	30	154	134	25	3.4	8.9	152	47.9%	.270
2019	NYM	MLB	28	11	10	0	32	30	160¹	163	27	2.9	8.6	153	46.3%	.304
2020	NYM	MLB	29	0	5	0	9	6	30²	42	14	2.9	10.6	36	33.3%	.346
2021 FS	TOR	MLB	30	9	8	0	26	26	150	143	22	3.0	9.2	152	43.4%	.299
2021 DC	TOR	MLB	30	8	7	0	22	22	127.7	122	19	3.0	9.2	130	43.4%	.299

Comparables: Andrew Heaney, Kevin Gausman, Anthony DeSclafani

Every time Matz threw a pitch in 2020, it seemed to be heading over the outfield wall. Giving up two home runs per nine innings is usually a cry for help, but Matz's rate of 4.11 homers per nine was so far beyond the pale that it dwarfed the numbers for every other starting pitcher in the league. Given that it's hardly possible for things to get worse from a performance perspective, and that he was a perfectly fine starter the two previous years, the Mets tendered him a contract for the 2021 season in the hopes that he can right the ship since his velocity and movement didn't change dramatically. If he can keep even a few more balls inside the stadium, he'll go back to being a decent starting pitcher—all the other tools are there.

YEAR	TEAM	LVL	AGE	WHIP	ERA	DRA-	WARP	MPH	FB%	WHF	CSP
2018	NYM	MLB	27	1.25	3.97	80	3.0	95.1	60.0%	23.3%	
2019	NYM	MLB	28	1.34	4.21	90	2.4	95.0	50.6%	23.0%	
2020	NYM	MLB	29	1.70	9.68	146	-0.5	96.1	53.9%	23.4%	
2021 FS	TOR	MLB	30	1.29	3.97	94	2.0	95.2	53.8%	23.2%	50.5%
2021 DC	TOR	MLB	30	1.29	3.97	94	1.6	95.2	53.8%	23.2%	50.5%

Steven Matz, continued

Pitch Shape vs LHH

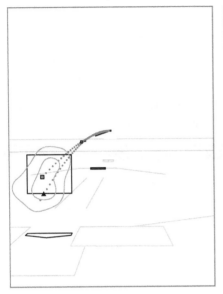

Pitch Shape vs RHH

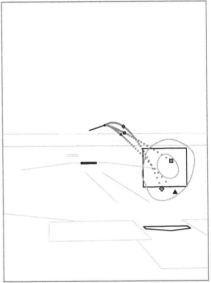

Type	Frequency	Velocity	H Movement	V Movement
□ Sinker	53.9%	94.6 [111]	13.3 [98]	-16.2 [114]
▲ Changeup	26.4%	85 [99]	14.6 [85]	-32.4 [86]
▽ Slider	4.7%	89.8 [126]	1.5 [74]	-25.7 [123]
◇ Curveball	15.0%	77.9 [97]	-12.6 [120]	-49.9 [97]

Julian Merryweather   RHP

Born: 10/14/91   Age: 29   Bats: R   Throws: R
Height: 6'4"   Weight: 215   Origin: Round 5, 2014 Draft (#158 overall)

YEAR	TEAM	LVL	AGE	W	L	SV	G	GS	IP	H	HR	BB/9	K/9	K	GB%	BABIP
2020	TOR	MLB	28	0	0	0	8	3	13	11	0	4.2	10.4	15	44.1%	.324
2021 FS	TOR	MLB	29	2	2	0	57	0	50	46	7	3.3	8.8	49	42.6%	.289
2021 DC	TOR	MLB	29	2	2	0	57	0	60	56	9	3.3	8.8	59	42.6%	.289

Comparables: Taylor Cole, Artie Lewicki, Jerad Eickhoff

Merryweather pitched 13 effective innings over eight games as a 29-year-old rookie, his velocity, pitch mix and ability to miss bats coming as a pleasant change of pace from Jays bullpens of recent years. But injury, his old enemy, found him once again, with elbow issues felling him before season's end.

YEAR	TEAM	LVL	AGE	WHIP	ERA	DRA-	WARP	MPH	FB%	WHF	CSP
2020	TOR	MLB	28	1.31	4.15	79	0.3	98.7	57.8%	26.1%	
2021 FS	TOR	MLB	29	1.30	4.05	95	0.4	98.7	57.8%	26.1%	48.4%
2021 DC	TOR	MLB	29	1.30	4.05	95	0.5	98.7	57.8%	26.1%	48.4%

Julian Merryweather, continued

Pitch Shape vs LHH

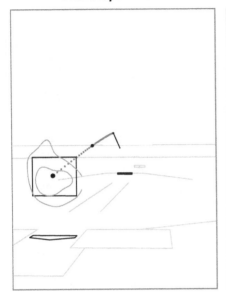

Pitch Shape vs RHH

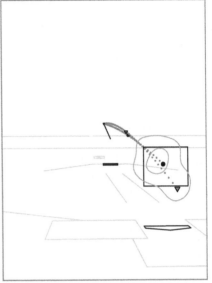

Type	Frequency	Velocity	H Movement	V Movement
● Fastball	57.5%	96.7 [113]	-6.4 [101]	-10.9 [112]
▲ Changeup	17.6%	80.6 [82]	-8.8 [116]	-28.9 [96]
▽ Slider	15.0%	85.9 [109]	1.3 [85]	-37.2 [90]
◇ Curveball	9.4%	79.3 [103]	6.2 [94]	-54 [88]

Nate Pearson   RHP

Born: 08/20/96   Age: 24   Bats: R   Throws: R
Height: 6'6"   Weight: 250   Origin: Round 1, 2017 Draft (#28 overall)

YEAR	TEAM	LVL	AGE	W	L	SV	G	GS	IP	H	HR	BB/9	K/9	K	GB%	BABIP
2018	DUN	HI-A	21	0	1	0	1	1	1^2	5	1	0.0	5.4	1	44.4%	.500
2019	DUN	HI-A	22	3	0	0	6	6	21	10	2	1.3	15.0	35	35.1%	.229
2019	NH	AA	22	1	4	0	16	16	62^2	41	4	3.0	9.9	69	38.8%	.250
2019	BUF	AAA	22	1	0	0	3	3	18	12	2	1.5	7.5	15	44.0%	.208
2020	TOR	MLB	23	1	0	0	5	4	18	14	5	6.5	8.0	16	38.5%	.191
2021 FS	TOR	MLB	24	9	8	0	26	26	150	139	25	4.4	9.5	157	38.5%	.291
2021 DC	TOR	MLB	24	7	7	0	24	24	121.3	113	20	4.4	9.5	127	38.5%	.291

Comparables: Mitch Keller, Marco Gonzales, Tyler Mahle

Pearson's debut was one of the most buzzed-about moments of the season for the Jays, and it didn't take long before it became clear what all the hype was about. The fastball, blazing, perfectly placed on the outside corner. The ridiculously hard slider. The velocity that only increased as the game went on. Unfortunately, the rest of the season wasn't as mind blowing as that debut. It was, in fact, a grind. Pearson seemed to lack the ease and confidence of his minor-league appearances, struggling with command of his pitches and failing to challenge hitters in a way that would play to his strengths. He made only four starts, the final two being very ugly indeed, before hitting the IL with a right flexor strain. But when he returned in relief during the final week of September, when the Jays bullpen was faltering, he was a breath of fresh air, a reminder of the hope that lies in a young team. He pitched two perfect innings during the Jays' last gasp against the Rays, striking out five, all swinging. Spring can't come soon enough.

YEAR	TEAM	LVL	AGE	WHIP	ERA	DRA-	WARP	MPH	FB%	WHF	CSP
2018	DUN	HI-A	21	3.00	10.80	40	0.1				
2019	DUN	HI-A	22	0.62	0.86	32	0.9				
2019	NH	AA	22	0.99	2.59	65	1.4				
2019	BUF	AAA	22	0.83	3.00	74	0.5				
2020	TOR	MLB	23	1.50	6.00	137	-0.2	99.4	50.6%	26.3%	
2021 FS	TOR	MLB	24	1.42	4.55	102	1.3	99.4	50.6%	26.3%	44.9%
2021 DC	TOR	MLB	24	1.42	4.55	102	1.0	99.4	50.6%	26.3%	44.9%

Nate Pearson, continued

Pitch Shape vs LHH

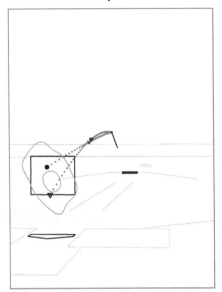

Pitch Shape vs RHH

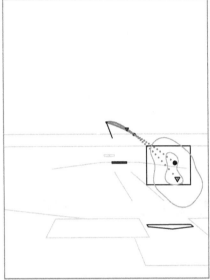

Type	Frequency	Velocity	H Movement	V Movement
● Fastball	50.6%	96.5 [112]	-5.6 [105]	-10.2 [114]
▲ Changeup	6.8%	87.8 [110]	-11.3 [102]	-23.4 [111]
▽ Slider	35.5%	84.7 [103]	5.9 [102]	-35.6 [95]
◇ Curveball	7.1%	77.5 [96]	9.8 [109]	-52.8 [90]

David Phelps RHP

Born: 10/09/86   Age: 34   Bats: R   Throws: R
Height: 6'2"   Weight: 198   Origin: Round 14, 2008 Draft (#440 overall)

YEAR	TEAM	LVL	AGE	W	L	SV	G	GS	IP	H	HR	BB/9	K/9	K	GB%	BABIP
2019	TOR	MLB	32	0	0	0	17	1	17^1	14	3	3.6	9.3	18	31.1%	.262
2019	CHC	MLB	32	2	1	1	24	0	17	17	2	5.3	9.5	18	45.8%	.326
2020	PHI	MLB	33	2	4	0	22	0	20^2	19	7	2.2	13.5	31	47.9%	.293
2021 FS	TOR	MLB	34	2	2	0	57	0	50	44	7	3.2	10.1	55	42.3%	.292

Comparables: Wade Davis, Brandon Morrow, Daniel Hudson

Seventeen times, Phelps threw a pitch that resulted in a flyball. Seven of those cleared the fence, and of those seven, six were left up; five topped 103 mph in exit velocity; four gave the opponents the lead; three lead to audible swearing on the broadcast; and two were described by broadcasters as moonshots. Two years removed from Tommy John, Phelps rediscovered his velocity but the command is in another castle. He's still worth a roster spot, but he might want to look for it somewhere besides Philadelphia.

YEAR	TEAM	LVL	AGE	WHIP	ERA	DRA-	WARP	MPH	FB%	WHF	CSP
2019	TOR	MLB	32	1.21	3.63	121	-0.1	93.6	39.7%	15.7%	
2019	CHC	MLB	32	1.59	3.18	99	0.1	94.6	45.5%	23.7%	
2020	PHI	MLB	33	1.16	6.53	78	0.4	95.3	46.5%	26.8%	
2021 FS	TOR	MLB	34	1.24	3.54	85	0.7	94.9	44.5%	23.2%	44.2%

David Phelps, continued

Pitch Shape vs LHH

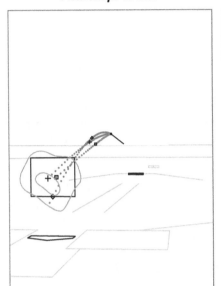

Pitch Shape vs RHH

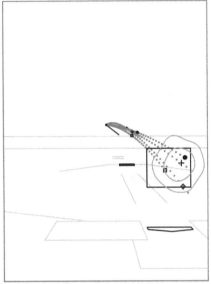

Type	Frequency	Velocity	H Movement	V Movement
● Fastball	22.4%	94.4 [106]	-7.6 [96]	-12.9 [106]
□ Sinker	24.1%	94.2 [109]	-13.9 [94]	-17.1 [111]
+ Cutter	26.9%	90.4 [113]	1.5 [97]	-19.5 [118]
◇ Curveball	26.6%	81.7 [112]	6.2 [95]	-45.9 [106]

Robbie Ray LHP

Born: 10/01/91   Age: 29   Bats: L   Throws: L
Height: 6'2"   Weight: 215   Origin: Round 12, 2010 Draft (#356 overall)

YEAR	TEAM	LVL	AGE	W	L	SV	G	GS	IP	H	HR	BB/9	K/9	K	GB%	BABIP
2018	ARI	MLB	26	6	2	0	24	24	123²	97	19	5.1	12.0	165	39.9%	.293
2019	ARI	MLB	27	12	8	0	33	33	174¹	150	30	4.3	12.1	235	36.6%	.315
2020	TOR	MLB	28	2	5	0	12	11	51²	53	13	7.8	11.8	68	24.8%	.323
2021 FS	TOR	MLB	29	9	9	0	26	26	150	132	26	5.2	11.6	193	34.7%	.303
2021 DC	TOR	MLB	29	8	8	0	25	25	134.7	119	23	5.2	11.6	174	34.7%	.303

Comparables: Jon Gray, A.J. Cole, Mike Foltynewicz

Ray allowed four or more walks in six of his 11 starts in 2020. He also struck out at least six in six of his 11 starts, but at what cost? Even his lone scoreless outing—his final start of the year against the Yankees—featured four walks, which is no way to live. When the Jays acquired him at the deadline from the Diamondbacks, there was some thought that they would be able to fix his free-pass problem. And, indeed, he didn't have any six-walk games with the Jays. (He had three such games with the D'Backs this year.) But he was inconsistent, with solid starts being followed by meltdowns, strikeouts being followed by inexplicable bouts of wildness. As he nears the age of 30, it's becoming clear that Ray's problem is just Ray himself, as with so many Bobby Witts before him. If nothing else, Ray's chaos was fitting for a year as chaotic 2020.

YEAR	TEAM	LVL	AGE	WHIP	ERA	DRA-	WARP	MPH	FB%	WHF	CSP
2018	ARI	MLB	26	1.35	3.93	89	1.9	95.9	54.0%	32.3%	
2019	ARI	MLB	27	1.34	4.34	83	3.2	94.4	52.8%	33.0%	
2020	TOR	MLB	28	1.90	6.62	183	-1.8	96.1	53.1%	33.0%	
2021 FS	TOR	MLB	29	1.46	4.68	104	1.1	95.2	53.1%	32.9%	44.5%
2021 DC	TOR	MLB	29	1.46	4.68	104	1.0	95.2	53.1%	32.9%	44.5%

Robbie Ray, continued

Pitch Shape vs LHH

Pitch Shape vs RHH

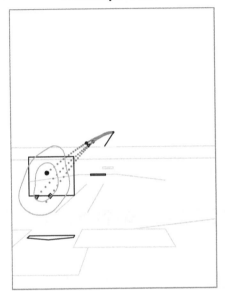
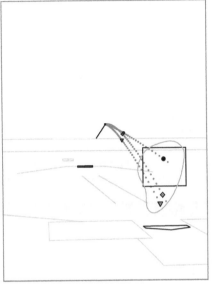

Type	Frequency	Velocity	H Movement	V Movement
● Fastball	51.2%	93.7 [104]	8.7 [90]	-13 [106]
▽ Slider	30.2%	86.6 [112]	0.1 [80]	-26.3 [121]
◇ Curveball	16.5%	83.6 [119]	-0.4 [71]	-36.9 [126]

Tanner Roark   RHP

Born: 10/05/86   Age: 34   Bats: R   Throws: R
Height: 6'2"   Weight: 238   Origin: Round 25, 2008 Draft (#753 overall)

YEAR	TEAM	LVL	AGE	W	L	SV	G	GS	IP	H	HR	BB/9	K/9	K	GB%	BABIP
2018	WAS	MLB	31	9	15	0	31	30	180¹	181	24	2.5	7.3	146	41.3%	.298
2019	CIN	MLB	32	6	7	0	21	21	110¹	119	14	3.1	8.7	107	36.5%	.332
2019	OAK	MLB	32	4	3	0	10	10	55	61	14	2.1	8.2	50	34.7%	.301
2020	TOR	MLB	33	2	3	0	11	11	47²	60	14	4.3	7.7	41	35.7%	.329
2021 FS	TOR	MLB	34	9	9	0	26	26	150	152	26	3.5	7.6	127	37.6%	.290
2021 DC	TOR	MLB	34	8	9	0	27	27	143	145	25	3.5	7.6	121	37.6%	.290

Comparables: Matt Shoemaker, Lance Lynn, Jake Arrieta

Wild, inconsistent, and very often hit hard, Roark starts for the Blue Jays were invariably bumpy rides. He struggled to throw strikes, and, when he did, had a tendency to serve up pitches that opponents could barrel. If there was one thing you could count on from Roark, it was that he wouldn't see the sixth inning; even his best starts were five-and-dives.

YEAR	TEAM	LVL	AGE	WHIP	ERA	DRA-	WARP	MPH	FB%	WHF	CSP
2018	WAS	MLB	31	1.28	4.34	109	0.9	93.3	59.2%	20.2%	
2019	CIN	MLB	32	1.42	4.24	108	0.6	94.1	52.4%	22.0%	
2019	OAK	MLB	32	1.35	4.58	137	-0.6	93.6	61.0%	21.0%	
2020	TOR	MLB	33	1.74	6.80	162	-1.2	92.8	53.3%	26.8%	
2021 FS	TOR	MLB	34	1.40	4.74	106	0.9	93.4	55.8%	22.5%	45.9%
2021 DC	TOR	MLB	34	1.40	4.74	106	0.9	93.4	55.8%	22.5%	45.9%

Tanner Roark, continued

Pitch Shape vs LHH

Pitch Shape vs RHH

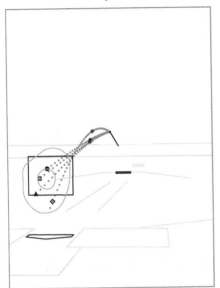
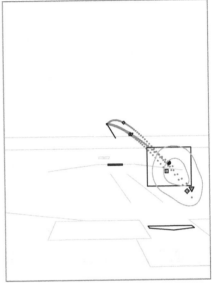

Type	Frequency	Velocity	H Movement	V Movement
● Fastball	33.5%	90.8 [94]	-3.8 [114]	-13.7 [104]
□ Sinker	19.8%	90.4 [90]	-10.7 [117]	-16.3 [114]
+ Cutter	3.6%	86.6 [89]	2.7 [105]	-20 [116]
▲ Changeup	13.4%	81 [84]	-8.8 [116]	-27.7 [99]
▽ Slider	15.0%	84 [100]	2.9 [91]	-28.9 [114]
◇ Curveball	14.8%	73.1 [79]	10.5 [112]	-60.6 [73]

Jordan Romano RHP

Born: 04/21/93   Age: 28   Bats: R   Throws: R
Height: 6'5"   Weight: 225   Origin: Round 10, 2014 Draft (#294 overall)

YEAR	TEAM	LVL	AGE	W	L	SV	G	GS	IP	H	HR	BB/9	K/9	K	GB%	BABIP
2018	NH	AA	25	11	8	0	25	25	137^1	122	15	2.7	8.2	125	36.7%	.281
2019	BUF	AAA	26	2	2	5	24	3	37^2	37	8	3.3	12.7	53	37.9%	.333
2019	TOR	MLB	26	0	2	0	17	0	15^1	17	4	5.3	12.3	21	48.8%	.351
2020	TOR	MLB	27	2	1	2	15	0	14^2	8	2	3.1	12.9	21	58.1%	.207
2021 FS	TOR	MLB	28	2	2	4	57	0	50	44	7	4.7	10.8	59	42.5%	.301
2021 DC	TOR	MLB	28	2	2	4	57	0	54	48	8	4.7	10.8	64	42.5%	.301

Comparables: Michael Feliz, Austin Brice, Keone Kela

There are few indisputable truths in this world, but one of them is that it's better to throw a 90 mph slider than an 85 mph one. Romero abandoned efforts to tinker with a changeup and poured his heart into his two pitches. He leaned on his new hard slider nearly 60 percent of the time, and the result was the third-best whiff rate in the American League (min. 10 IP). The pitch actually gained average velocity as the season went on. A finger injury kept him out of the postseason, but with Ken Giles no longer in the picture, the past future closer is back to being the present future closer, and a near-perfect one at that.

YEAR	TEAM	LVL	AGE	WHIP	ERA	DRA-	WARP	MPH	FB%	WHF	CSP
2018	NH	AA	25	1.19	4.13	104	0.6				
2019	BUF	AAA	26	1.35	5.73	87	0.8				
2019	TOR	MLB	26	1.70	7.63	83	0.2	97.0	63.7%	29.5%	
2020	TOR	MLB	27	0.89	1.23	70	0.4	98.3	40.3%	43.8%	
2021 FS	TOR	MLB	28	1.42	4.45	99	0.3	97.7	51.2%	37.1%	45.3%
2021 DC	TOR	MLB	28	1.42	4.45	99	0.3	97.7	51.2%	37.1%	45.3%

Jordan Romano, continued

Pitch Shape vs LHH

Pitch Shape vs RHH

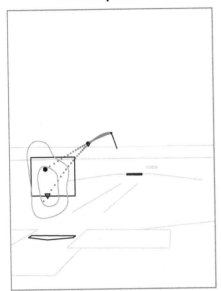 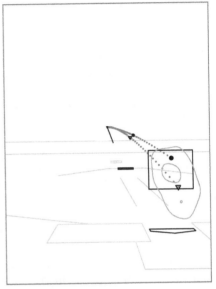

Type	Frequency	Velocity	H Movement	V Movement
● Fastball	40.3%	96.7 [113]	-5.1 [108]	-11 [112]
▽ Slider	59.7%	89.3 [124]	3.2 [92]	-30.5 [109]

Hyun Jin Ryu   LHP

Born: 03/25/87   Age: 34   Bats: R   Throws: L
Height: 6'3"   Weight: 255   Origin: International Free Agent, 2013

YEAR	TEAM	LVL	AGE	W	L	SV	G	GS	IP	H	HR	BB/9	K/9	K	GB%	BABIP
2018	LAD	MLB	31	7	3	0	15	15	82¹	68	9	1.6	9.7	89	45.7%	.282
2019	LAD	MLB	32	14	5	0	29	29	182²	160	17	1.2	8.0	163	49.6%	.282
2020	TOR	MLB	33	5	2	0	12	12	67	60	6	2.3	9.7	72	50.8%	.303
2021 FS	TOR	MLB	34	10	7	0	26	26	150	138	18	2.3	9.0	149	50.2%	.295
2021 DC	TOR	MLB	34	11	7	0	27	27	159.7	147	19	2.3	9.0	159	50.2%	.295

Comparables: Matt Shoemaker, Johnny Cueto, Felix Hernandez

It was a pleasant surprise when Ryu signed a four-year deal with the Jays last offseason. It was no surprise that he was the Jays' most valuable pitcher by far in 2020. His first couple of starts were shaky, prompting some classic Jays fan sky-is-falling catastrophizing, but proved to be nothing more than rust. After August began, Ryu never failed to complete five innings, despite contending with some shaky defense behind him. Often he worked into the seventh, his turns a consistently welcome reprieve for the many overworked relievers in the Jays bullpen. He managed contact better than pretty much anyone. The story was marred by his lone postseason start, a cacophony of diminished velocity and missed spots, a warrior beaten. But with an actual ace on the team for the first time in years, there's reason to hope that Ryu will be able to make up for that late-September failure in the not-so-distant future.

Where the young position players on his team are known for their ebullience, Ryu brought a quieter, more stabilizing sense of joy to the team. He became an aficionado of the bright, updated powder blues introduced to the Jays' wardrobe this season; along with interpreter Bryan Lee, he was a fixture in the dugout. The key to happiness in life is balance.

YEAR	TEAM	LVL	AGE	WHIP	ERA	DRA-	WARP	MPH	FB%	WHF	CSP
2018	LAD	MLB	31	1.01	1.97	54	2.7	92.1	37.0%	27.5%	
2019	LAD	MLB	32	1.01	2.32	62	5.4	92.6	40.6%	24.9%	
2020	TOR	MLB	33	1.15	2.69	74	1.5	91.6	34.7%	26.3%	
2021 FS	TOR	MLB	34	1.18	3.19	79	3.2	92.2	38.2%	25.7%	47.6%
2021 DC	TOR	MLB	34	1.18	3.19	79	3.4	92.2	38.2%	25.7%	47.6%

Hyun Jin Ryu, continued

Pitch Shape vs LHH

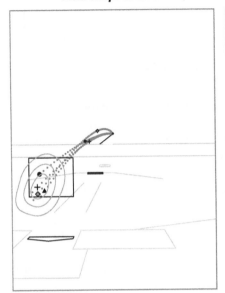

Pitch Shape vs RHH

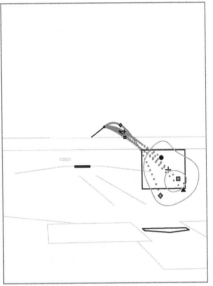

Type	Frequency	Velocity	H Movement	V Movement
● Fastball	23.8%	89.9 [92]	8.6 [91]	-18.2 [92]
□ Sinker	11.0%	89.2 [83]	13.8 [95]	-22.5 [94]
+ Cutter	24.3%	85.6 [83]	-1.3 [96]	-26.9 [90]
▲ Changeup	27.8%	79.7 [79]	11.8 [99]	-33 [85]
◇ Curveball	13.2%	72.4 [76]	-11.7 [117]	-60.1 [74]

Matt Shoemaker RHP

Born: 09/27/86   Age: 34   Bats: R   Throws: R
Height: 6'2"   Weight: 225   Origin: Undrafted Free Agent, 2008

YEAR	TEAM	LVL	AGE	W	L	SV	G	GS	IP	H	HR	BB/9	K/9	K	GB%	BABIP
2018	LAA	MLB	31	2	2	0	7	7	31	29	3	2.9	9.6	33	43.0%	.313
2019	TOR	MLB	32	3	0	0	5	5	28²	16	3	2.8	7.5	24	51.4%	.183
2020	TOR	MLB	33	0	1	0	6	6	28²	22	8	2.8	8.2	26	50.0%	.197
2021 FS	TOR	MLB	34	2	2	0	57	0	50	47	7	2.7	8.4	46	45.0%	.286
2021 DC	TOR	MLB	34	6	5	0	19	19	97	91	14	2.7	8.4	91	45.0%	.286

Comparables: Tanner Roark, Ian Kennedy, Homer Bailey

Shoemaker's 2019 season, which started out with a series of dominant outings, was tragically cut short by injury: a freak accident covering a play on the bases, leaving him with a torn ACL. He ended the year having thrown just 28⅔ innings. Hopes were high for a comeback, but Shoemaker ended 2020 having thrown, again, 28⅔ innings. It was injury that slowed him down once more; this time, not a random one, but a persistent shoulder inflammation that hampered his performance when he was on the mound. He was beset by home runs, and most of his appearances were belabored. That wasn't the case for his appearance in the postseason, though, where he pitched a sparkling three innings against the eventual pennant-winning Rays. Before the game, the controversy was that Shoemaker was the one being handed the ball; afterward, the controversy was that it had been taken away from him so early. This is something that Shoemaker has managed to do again and again in his career: come back, prove people wrong. But he's getting older now, and the mid-30s are not a kind age for pitchers with an ever-growing list of injuries behind them.

YEAR	TEAM	LVL	AGE	WHIP	ERA	DRA-	WARP	MPH	FB%	WHF	CSP
2018	LAA	MLB	31	1.26	4.94	125	-0.1	93.8	47.1%	28.8%	
2019	TOR	MLB	32	0.87	1.57	93	0.4	92.7	46.7%	28.5%	
2020	TOR	MLB	33	1.08	4.71	103	.0.2	94.1	44.2%	28.5%	
2021 FS	TOR	MLB	34	1.25	3.89	94	0.4	93.6	45.5%	28.6%	46.6%
2021 DC	TOR	MLB	34	1.25	3.89	94	1.2	93.6	45.5%	28.6%	46.6%

Matt Shoemaker, continued

Pitch Shape vs LHH

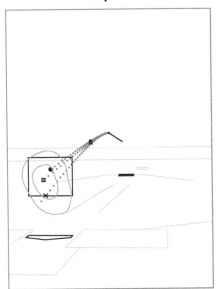

Pitch Shape vs RHH

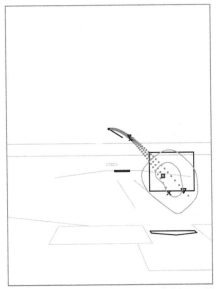

Type	Frequency	Velocity	H Movement	V Movement
● Fastball	18.6%	92.3 [99]	-7.3 [97]	-14 [103]
□ Sinker	25.6%	92.2 [99]	-14.2 [92]	-19.5 [103]
✕ Splitter	32.5%	85.6 [102]	-9.2 [95]	-29.5 [100]
▽ Slider	18.4%	81.6 [90]	4.9 [99]	-35.6 [95]
◇ Curveball	4.9%	75.7 [89]	9.7 [109]	-45.3 [107]

Ross Stripling   RHP

Born: 11/23/89   Age: 31   Bats: R   Throws: R
Height: 6'3"   Weight: 220   Origin: Round 5, 2012 Draft (#176 overall)

YEAR	TEAM	LVL	AGE	W	L	SV	G	GS	IP	H	HR	BB/9	K/9	K	GB%	BABIP
2018	LAD	MLB	28	8	6	0	33	21	122	123	18	1.6	10.0	136	45.3%	.324
2019	LAD	MLB	29	4	4	0	32	15	90²	84	11	2.0	9.2	93	49.8%	.299
2020	TOR	MLB	30	3	3	1	12	9	49¹	56	13	3.3	7.3	40	40.4%	.295
2021 FS	TOR	MLB	31	10	7	0	26	26	150	141	22	2.4	8.1	135	45.1%	.284
2021 DC	TOR	MLB	31	8	4	0	24	12	108	102	16	2.4	8.1	97	45.1%	.284

Comparables: Matt Andriese, Raisel Iglesias, Kelvin Herrera

Grizzled coaches used to yell at their struggling starters to "just throw strikes," and now we have proof they were full of it. After struggling with the Dodgers in the first half of the season, the Jays picked up Stripling at the deadline to bolster their rotation, with the hopes that a change of scenery and more playing time might help ease his woes. It didn't. Stripling, in his five September games with the Jays, got hit hard, when he wasn't struggling with walks; this despite the fact that he was actually throwing more pitches in the zone than ever. The problem: His curveball simply didn't generate the whiffs it needs to for Stripling to thrive, and the man clearly knew it, nearly abandoning it for the slider after switching teams. He'll need to find the old magic, because unless he can get batters to chase, strike two will hold no fear over batters.

YEAR	TEAM	LVL	AGE	WHIP	ERA	DRA-	WARP	MPH	FB%	WHF	CSP
2018	LAD	MLB	28	1.19	3.02	65	3.3	93.8	41.1%	26.0%	
2019	LAD	MLB	29	1.15	3.47	71	2.2	92.7	39.0%	24.5%	
2020	TOR	MLB	30	1.50	5.84	134	-0.4	93.8	43.9%	18.9%	
2021 FS	TOR	MLB	31	1.21	3.56	86	2.6	93.3	41.2%	23.0%	48.4%
2021 DC	TOR	MLB	31	1.21	3.56	86	1.8	93.3	41.2%	23.0%	48.4%

Ross Stripling, continued

Pitch Shape vs LHH

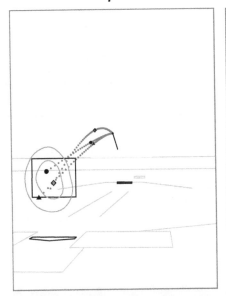

Pitch Shape vs RHH

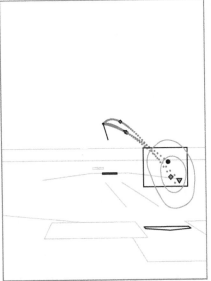

Type	Frequency	Velocity	H Movement	V Movement
● Fastball	43.7%	91.7 [97]	-4.5 [111]	-13 [106]
▲ Changeup	17.3%	84.6 [98]	-10.1 [108]	-26.6 [102]
▽ Slider	14.8%	85.8 [108]	4.5 [97]	-30.3 [110]
◇ Curveball	23.9%	78.7 [100]	3.9 [85]	-54.5 [86]

Jacob Waguespack RHP

Born: 11/05/93   Age: 27   Bats: R   Throws: R
Height: 6'6"   Weight: 235   Origin: Round 37, 2012 Draft (#1126 overall)

YEAR	TEAM	LVL	AGE	W	L	SV	G	GS	IP	H	HR	BB/9	K/9	K	GB%	BABIP
2018	REA	AA	24	1	1	0	7	7	29¹	31	0	4.9	9.5	31	56.8%	.352
2018	LHV	AAA	24	3	5	1	14	8	53¹	54	4	3.4	8.1	48	50.9%	.323
2018	BUF	AAA	24	2	4	0	7	6	39¹	47	3	2.3	7.6	33	51.5%	.349
2019	BUF	AAA	25	2	6	0	12	11	52²	57	9	4.3	8.9	52	47.1%	.327
2019	TOR	MLB	25	5	5	0	16	13	78	75	12	3.3	7.3	63	40.8%	.279
2020	TOR	MLB	26	0	0	0	11	0	17²	27	2	4.6	8.2	16	41.3%	.410
2021 FS	TOR	MLB	27	2	2	0	57	0	50	48	8	3.8	8.0	44	42.7%	.283
2021 DC	TOR	MLB	27	1	1	0	26	0	36	34	6	3.8	8.0	32	42.7%	.283

Comparables: Chase De Jong, Erick Fedde, Brian Matusz

After starting the season with a string of scoreless outings, Waguespack saw his 2020 slide downhill. At first it was a slow trickle: a run allowed here, an error-induced disaster. But in his final three appearances of the season, Waguespack allowed 15 runs (11 earned) in just over six innings, adding up to a very ugly line when everything was accounted for. One of the awkward modern mechanisms of baseball is when a long reliever goes multiple innings and gets rewarded with a drive to Triple-A for the sake of a fresh arm; at least Waguespack made things easier by providing a decent excuse.

YEAR	TEAM	LVL	AGE	WHIP	ERA	DRA-	WARP	MPH	FB%	WHF	CSP
2018	REA	AA	24	1.60	3.99	95	0.3				
2018	LHV	AAA	24	1.39	5.06	89	0.6				
2018	BUF	AAA	24	1.45	5.03	92	0.4				
2019	BUF	AAA	25	1.56	5.30	110	0.7				
2019	TOR	MLB	25	1.33	4.38	116	0.0	94.2	72.8%	21.8%	
2020	TOR	MLB	26	2.04	8.15	100	0.2	94.1	68.2%	24.7%	
2021 FS	TOR	MLB	27	1.39	4.52	103	0.2	94.2	71.4%	22.7%	45.9%
2021 DC	TOR	MLB	27	1.39	4.52	103	0.2	94.2	71.4%	22.7%	45.9%

Jacob Waguespack, continued

Pitch Shape vs LHH   Pitch Shape vs RHH

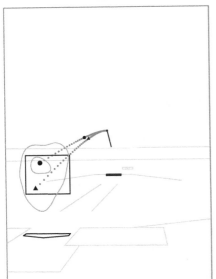 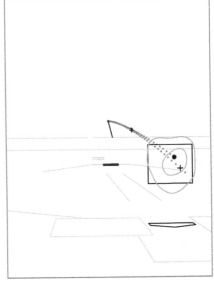

Type	Frequency	Velocity	H Movement	V Movement
● Fastball	43.3%	92.6 [100]	-1.7 [124]	-13.1 [106]
▢ Sinker	8.3%	91.2 [93]	-.9 [130]	-15.1 [117]
+ Cutter	16.4%	88.9 [103]	2.5 [104]	-21.7 [110]
▲ Changeup	18.9%	82.3 [89]	-7.4 [123]	-27.6 [100]
◇ Curveball	10.8%	75.8 [89]	2.8 [81]	-49.4 [98]

Taijuan Walker   RHP

Born: 08/13/92   Age: 28   Bats: R   Throws: R
Height: 6'4"   Weight: 235   Origin: Round 1, 2010 Draft (#43 overall)

YEAR	TEAM	LVL	AGE	W	L	SV	G	GS	IP	H	HR	BB/9	K/9	K	GB%	BABIP
2018	ARI	MLB	25	0	0	0	3	3	13	15	1	3.5	6.2	9	40.5%	.341
2019	ARI	MLB	26	0	0	0	1	1	1	1	0	0.0	9.0	1	33.3%	.333
2020	TOR	MLB	27	4	3	0	11	11	53¹	43	8	3.2	8.4	50	38.2%	.243
2021 FS	TOR	MLB	28	9	8	0	26	26	150	143	25	3.3	8.5	142	40.3%	.287
2021 DC	TOR	MLB	28	5	5	0	16	16	79.3	75	13	3.3	8.5	75	40.3%	.287

Comparables: Julio Teheran, Shelby Miller, Chad Kuhl

For the first time in years, the Jays were buyers at the trade deadline, and their major area of need was obvious: starting pitching. So they acquired Walker, one of the better options out there, for a single shiny lottery ticket, sending Rookie-level outfielder Alberto Rodríguez to Seattle. Through his five starts in Seattle to open the season, Walker didn't have eye-popping numbers, but he was averaging more than five innings per start, length that the overtaxed bullpen desperately needed. In terms of results, the trade worked out swimmingly for the Jays, with Walker having one of the best September of any starting pitcher in baseball by ERA. Based on his peripherals, Walker will make for a risky acquisition for some ballclub over the winter, though his age, former prospect pedigree and growing distance from Tommy John all provide some reason for optimism.

YEAR	TEAM	LVL	AGE	WHIP	ERA	DRA-	WARP	MPH	FB%	WHF	CSP
2018	ARI	MLB	25	1.54	3.46	115	0.0	96.0	70.5%	18.8%	
2019	ARI	MLB	26	1.00	0.00			94.0	66.7%	20.0%	
2020	TOR	MLB	27	1.16	2.70	99	0.5	94.8	50.2%	20.5%	
2021 FS	TOR	MLB	28	1.32	4.42	100	1.4	94.9	51.9%	20.4%	48.5%
2021 DC	TOR	MLB	28	1.32	4.42	100	0.8	94.9	51.9%	20.4%	48.5%

Taijuan Walker, continued

Pitch Shape vs LHH

Pitch Shape vs RHH

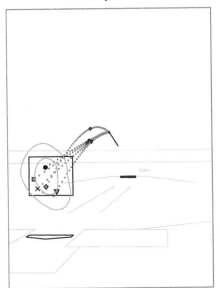
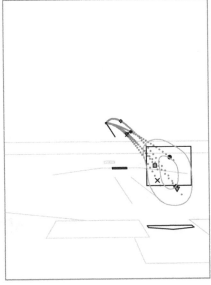

Type	Frequency	Velocity	H Movement	V Movement
● Fastball	37.7%	93.3 [102]	-6 [103]	-11.9 [109]
□ Sinker	12.3%	93.1 [103]	-12.8 [102]	-16.1 [114]
✕ Splitter	18.1%	89.1 [118]	-12.1 [84]	-23.3 [120]
▽ Slider	21.5%	85.3 [106]	4.4 [97]	-30.2 [110]
◇ Curveball	10.1%	74.7 [85]	8.4 [103]	-59 [76]

Shun Yamaguchi   RHP

Born: 07/11/87   Age: 33   Bats: R   Throws: R
Height: 6'2"   Weight: 225   Origin: International Free Agent, 2019

YEAR	TEAM	LVL	AGE	W	L	SV	G	GS	IP	H	HR	BB/9	K/9	K	GB%	BABIP
2020	TOR	MLB	32	2	4	0	17	0	25²	28	6	6.0	9.1	26	38.7%	.319
2021 FS	TOR	MLB	33	2	3	0	57	0	50	46	7	4.8	9.1	50	39.6%	.291
2021 DC	TOR	MLB	33	6	5	0	57	6	62	58	9	4.8	9.1	62	39.6%	.291

In his final outing of the season, Yamaguchi gave up three home runs over the course of a few innings in a Blue Jays blowout—a fitting end to an inconsistent season. The former NPB strikeout leader had an extremely inauspicious start to his MLB career: His first appearances were all in runner-on-second 10th innings, and they were all unmitigated disasters. His subsequent appearances were largely unremarkable, which is exactly what one wants out of middle relief, though even then his pitch maps bear a striking resemblance to a shotgun blast. But it's the memory of his first games, of the flat, slow pitches, the strike-zone nibbling, that still lingers, sometimes as more than a memory. Trust is easy to lose, but so hard to regain.

YEAR	TEAM	LVL	AGE	WHIP	ERA	DRA-	WARP	MPH	FB%	WHF	CSP
2020	TOR	MLB	32	1.75	8.06	131	-0.2	93.0	41.0%	28.3%	
2021 FS	TOR	MLB	33	1.47	4.69	109	0.0	93.0	41.0%	28.3%	44.2%
2021 DC	TOR	MLB	33	1.47	4.69	109	0.0	93.0	41.0%	28.3%	44.2%

Shun Yamaguchi, continued

Pitch Shape vs LHH

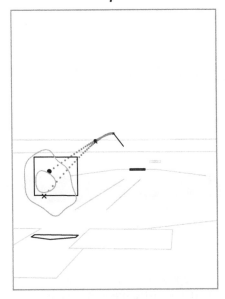

Pitch Shape vs RHH

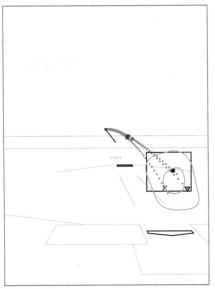

Type	Frequency	Velocity	H Movement	V Movement
● Fastball	40.8%	90.8 [94]	-9.7 [85]	-15.9 [98]
✕ Splitter	39.8%	84.8 [98]	-9.8 [93]	-31.5 [93]
▽ Slider	16.5%	81.7 [90]	4.6 [97]	-33.5 [101]

PLAYER COMMENTS WITHOUT GRAPHS

Riley Adams C

Born: 06/26/96 Age: 25 Bats: R Throws: R
Height: 6'4" Weight: 235 Origin: Round 3, 2017 Draft (#99 overall)

YEAR	TEAM	LVL	AGE	PA	R	2B	3B	HR	RBI	BB	K	SB	CS	AVG/OBP/SLG
2018	DUN	HI-A	22	409	49	26	1	4	43	50	93	3	0	.246/.352/.361
2019	DUN	HI-A	23	83	12	3	0	3	12	14	18	1	0	.277/.434/.462
2019	NH	AA	23	332	46	15	2	11	39	32	105	3	1	.258/.349/.439
2021 FS	TOR	MLB	25	600	57	23	1	15	60	47	200	0	0	.208/.285/.342

Comparables: Adrian Nieto, Dusty Ryan, Jacob Stallings

After getting into but a single, ill-fated game in 2019, Diaz entered camp in 2020 competing for the fifth starter spot. He left it quickly, straining a lat in March and spending the summer on

YEAR	TEAM	P. COUNT	FRM RUNS	BLK RUNS	THRW RUNS	TOT RUNS
2021	TOR	16650	-4.8	2.6	0.0	-2.2
2021	TOR	16650	-4.8	3.6	0.0	-1.2

the 60-day IL. Since he seems to be destined for a bullpen role without a serviceable, battle-tested changeup, his development was among the most jeopardized by the pandemic-shortened, minor-league-less season.

YEAR	TEAM	LVL	AGE	PA	DRC+	BABIP	BRR	FRAA	WARP
2018	DUN	HI-A	22	409	121	.323	-1.3	C(93): 4.3, 1B(1): -0.0	2.2
2019	DUN	HI-A	23	83	168	.341	0.4	C(19): 0.1	1.0
2019	NH	AA	23	332	131	.362	1.0	C(57): -2.5	2.1
2021 FS	TOR	MLB	25	600	73	.300	-0.9	C -1, 1B 0	0.2

Jordan Groshans SS

Born: 11/10/99   Age: 21   Bats: R   Throws: R
Height: 6'3"   Weight: 205   Origin: Round 1, 2018 Draft (#12 overall)

YEAR	TEAM	LVL	AGE	PA	R	2B	3B	HR	RBI	BB	K	SB	CS	AVG/OBP/SLG
2018	BLU	ROK	18	48	4	1	0	1	4	2	8	0	0	.182/.229/.273
2018	BLU	ROK	18	159	17	12	0	4	39	13	29	0	0	.331/.390/.500
2019	LAN	LO-A	19	96	12	6	0	2	13	13	21	1	1	.337/.427/.482
2021 FS	TOR	MLB	21	600	48	22	1	9	51	38	181	1	1	.207/.263/.306

Comparables: Carter Kieboom, Corey Seager, Rowdy Tellez

"Quit making excuses and get better. There's literally nothing to do in this time but to get better. It's not a vacation." If Groshans' Twitter proverbs are any indication, the pandemic and the cancellation of the minor league season haven't slowed him down a bit. The arrival of 2020 draft choice Austin Martin may have completed Groshans' inevitable transition to third, but there's little concern over whether he can handle the position offensively or defensively. The foot injury that cut his breakout 2019 short is fully healed, and the six home runs he hit in spring training 2.0 hinted at a promise to come.

YEAR	TEAM	LVL	AGE	PA	DRC+	BABIP	BRR	FRAA	WARP
2018	BLU	ROK	18	48		.194			
2018	BLU	ROK	18	159		.387			
2019	LAN	LO-A	19	96	169	.433	-0.4	SS(20): -1.8	0.9
2021 FS	TOR	MLB	21	600	56	.289	-0.8	SS 1, 3B -1	-1.9

Miguel Hiraldo   3B

Born: 09/05/00   Age: 20   Bats: R   Throws: R
Height: 5'11"   Weight: 170   Origin: International Free Agent, 2017

YEAR	TEAM	LVL	AGE	PA	R	2B	3B	HR	RBI	BB	K	SB	CS	AVG/OBP/SLG
2018	DSL BLJ	ROK	17	239	41	18	3	2	33	23	30	15	6	.313/.381/.453
2018	BLU	ROK	17	40	3	4	0	0	3	1	12	3	0	.231/.250/.333
2019	BLU	ROK+	18	256	43	20	1	7	37	14	36	11	3	.300/.348/.481
2019	LAN	LO-A	18	4	0	0	1	0	0	0	0	0	0	.250/.250/.750
2021 FS	TOR	MLB	20	600	44	23	2	8	49	28	162	16	6	.206/.247/.299

Comparables: J.P. Crawford, Estevan Florial, Ramón Flores

Hiraldo used to play the same position as Vladimir Guerrero, Jr.; now he just plays the same position as vaunted prospect Orelvis Martinez. This is the problem with focusing on ordinal prospect lists; in a lesser system, his angry bat and advanced progression would be driving anticipation, but with the Blue Jays he's the fallback for bigger dreams. There's some question defensively about his stocky build, but the good news is that his bat will carry him as far down the defensive spectrum as he needs to go. Hiraldo can hit, and if he continues to do so, that'll be enough, either for Toronto or whichever team takes advantage of their surplus.

YEAR	TEAM	LVL	AGE	PA	DRC+	BABIP	BRR	FRAA	WARP
2018	DSL BLJ	ROK	17	239		.355			
2018	BLU	ROK	17	40		.333			
2019	BLU	ROK+	18	256		.328			
2019	LAN	LO-A	18	4	79	.250	0.0	2B(1): 0.0	0.0
2021 FS	TOR	MLB	20	600	48	.274	1.4	SS 4, 3B 0	-1.7

Alejandro Kirk   C

Born: 11/06/98   Age: 22   Bats: R   Throws: R
Height: 5'8"   Weight: 265   Origin: International Free Agent, 2016

YEAR	TEAM	LVL	AGE	PA	R	2B	3B	HR	RBI	BB	K	SB	CS	AVG/OBP/SLG
2018	BLU	ROK	19	244	31	10	1	10	57	33	21	2	0	.354/.443/.558
2019	LAN	LO-A	20	96	15	6	1	3	8	18	8	1	0	.299/.427/.519
2019	DUN	HI-A	20	276	26	25	0	4	36	38	31	2	0	.288/.395/.446
2020	TOR	MLB	21	25	4	2	0	1	3	1	4	0	0	.375/.400/.583
2021 FS	TOR	MLB	22	600	76	31	1	14	67	54	105	0	0	.256/.330/.400
2021 DC	TOR	MLB	22	154	19	8	0	3	17	14	27	0	0	.256/.330/.400

Comparables: Luis Campusano, Logan Morrison, Chance Sisco

Kirk provided the natural evolution of one trend, and the subversion of another. You can't talk about the young catcher/designated hitter without mentioning his size, of course;

YEAR	TEAM	P. COUNT	FRM RUNS	BLK RUNS	THRW RUNS	TOT RUNS
2020	TOR	1001	-0.6	0.0	0.0	-0.6
2021	TOR	3608	-2.1	0.6	0.0	-1.5
2021	TOR	3608	-2.1	0.2	0.0	-1.9

if his Vogelbachian predecessors were sometimes described as bowling balls, Kirk is a cannonball. That said, his offensive profile is more akin to Willians Astudillo, demonstrating a short swing and excellent bat-to-ball skills, as well as credible blocking and framing skills given his own frame. Where he, and many other prospects, bucked a trend in 2020 is by jumping from A-ball to apply those skills. The Blue Jays, in the thick of a pennant race, wisely decided that if Kirk's lack of athleticism was going to be a problem in the future, they may as well take advantage of the present. A four-hit, triple-shy-of-the-cycle performance on September 21 was his exclamation point, but he only went one start, and that a seven-inning affair, without getting at least one hit. He'll be fun to watch in 2021.

YEAR	TEAM	LVL	AGE	PA	DRC+	BABIP	BRR	FRAA	WARP
2018	BLU	ROK	19	244		.354			
2019	LAN	LO-A	20	96	162	.299	0.9	C(17): 0.1	1.1
2019	DUN	HI-A	20	276	153	.317	-3.4	C(68): 0.8	2.4
2020	TOR	MLB	21	25	96	.421	-0.3	C(7): -0.1	0.0
2021 FS	TOR	MLB	22	600	100	.296	-0.9	C -4	2.0
2021 DC	TOR	MLB	22	154	100	.296	-0.2	C -1	0.3

Austin Martin   SS

Born: 03/23/99   Age: 22   Bats: R   Throws: R
Height: 6'0"   Weight: 185   Origin: Round 1, 2020 Draft (#5 overall)

Widely considered the best pure hitter in the draft, Toronto was pleasantly surprised to see the former Vanderbilt standout fall to the fifth pick. Despite not being able to jump into a minor-league season, reports from Rochester were glowing on both sides of the ball. Martin did fielding work at infield and outfield positions, and his natural hitting ability and advanced approach are building anticipation for the day when he can actually play in a minor-league game. If there's any cause for caution here, it's the occasional assumption that growth is automatic; Martin could develop power and become one of the league's best hitters, or he could hit a lot of pleasant, sharp line drives over the infielders.

Orelvis Martinez SS

Born: 11/19/01   Age: 19   Bats: R   Throws: R
Height: 6'1"   Weight: 188   Origin: International Free Agent, 2018

YEAR	TEAM	LVL	AGE	PA	R	2B	3B	HR	RBI	BB	K	SB	CS	AVG/OBP/SLG
2019	BLU	ROK	17	163	20	8	5	7	32	14	29	2	0	.275/.352/.549
2021 FS	TOR	MLB	19	600	43	19	3	8	48	31	187	2	1	.191/.240/.282

Comparables: Anderson Tejeda, Yu Chang, Corey Seager

Martinez's 2020 season was one of the most anticipated among Jays prospect-watchers. The teenager with the explosive power was to enter his first full year as a pro—but, of course, that didn't happen. Instead of providing crucial developmental data, Martinez and his fellow Latin American teenagers spent the early stages of quarantine outside a Florida hotel, hitting and throwing balled socks wrapped in tape. Our eager eyes shall have to wait until (hopefully) the spring, when it will become more clear whether he can channel the chaos of his swing into consistent production against higher-level pitching, and non-footwear equipment.

YEAR	TEAM	LVL	AGE	PA	DRC+	BABIP	BRR	FRAA	WARP
2019	BLU	ROK	17	163		.296			
2021 FS	TOR	MLB	19	600	42	.270	0.0	SS -4, 3B -1	-3.5

Reese McGuire C

Born: 03/02/95   Age: 26   Bats: L   Throws: R
Height: 6'0"   Weight: 215   Origin: Round 1, 2013 Draft (#14 overall)

YEAR	TEAM	LVL	AGE	PA	R	2B	3B	HR	RBI	BB	K	SB	CS	AVG/OBP/SLG
2018	BUF	AAA	23	369	31	9	2	7	37	33	77	3	2	.233/.312/.339
2018	TOR	MLB	23	33	5	3	0	2	4	2	9	1	0	.290/.333/.581
2019	BUF	AAA	24	277	30	12	1	5	29	25	44	4	0	.247/.316/.366
2019	TOR	MLB	24	105	14	7	0	5	11	7	18	0	0	.299/.346/.526
2020	TOR	MLB	25	45	2	0	0	1	1	0	11	0	0	.073/.073/.146
2021 FS	TOR	MLB	26	600	68	22	1	16	63	47	124	2	1	.225/.293/.361
2021 DC	TOR	MLB	26	185	21	7	0	4	19	14	38	0	0	.225/.293/.361

Comparables: Justin Knoedler, Bryan Holaday, George Kottaras

That could certainly have gone better. McGuire opened camp in unique fashion, getting arrested for some extracurricular automotive activity—if you know thyself, you know thyself—and providing ballpark organists around the country with a lifetime of musical ammunition. He proceeded to hand back two seasons'

YEAR	TEAM	P. COUNT	FRM RUNS	BLK RUNS	THRW RUNS	TOT RUNS
2018	TOR	1370	0.4	0.5	-0.1	0.9
2018	BUF	9722	15.4	0.2	0.3	15.8
2019	TOR	4094	5.0	0.4	0.0	5.4
2019	BUF	10274	7.0	0.0	-1.5	5.5
2020	TOR	1815	-0.4	0.1	0.0	-0.2
2021	TOR	7215	4.4	2.0	0.2	6.5
2021	TOR	7215	4.4	1.5	0.2	6.0

worth of surprising offensive production in one concentrated supply of weapons-grade regression. Those details, combined with the sudden arrival of theoretical catching prospect Alejandro Kirk, dealt a sizable blow to any dreams of working his way into a short-side platoon with starter Danny Jansen. McGuire's defensive acumen, and his lack of options, will keep him in the Blue Jays' plans for a little longer, but only just.

YEAR	TEAM	LVL	AGE	PA	DRC+	BABIP	BRR	FRAA	WARP
2018	BUF	AAA	23	369	94	.281	1.6	C(73): 15.0	2.4
2018	TOR	MLB	23	33	95	.350	0.3	C(11): 0.7	0.2
2019	BUF	AAA	24	277	77	.276	-3.8	C(71): 4.2	0.7
2019	TOR	MLB	24	105	106	.324	0.6	C(30): 5.0	1.2
2020	TOR	MLB	25	45	54	.069	-0.5	C(18): 0.0	-0.2
2021 FS	TOR	MLB	26	600	77	.263	-0.7	C 15	2.2
2021 DC	TOR	MLB	26	185	77	.263	-0.2	C 6	0.8

Gabriel Moreno   C

Born: 02/14/00   Age: 21   Bats: R   Throws: R
Height: 5'11"   Weight: 160   Origin: International Free Agent, 2016

YEAR	TEAM	LVL	AGE	PA	R	2B	3B	HR	RBI	BB	K	SB	CS	AVG/OBP/SLG
2018	BLU	ROK	18	101	14	12	2	2	22	4	7	1	1	.413/.455/.652
2018	BLU	ROK	18	66	10	5	0	2	14	3	13	1	0	.279/.303/.459
2019	LAN	LO-A	19	341	47	17	5	12	52	22	38	7	1	.280/.337/.485
2021 FS	TOR	MLB	21	600	54	26	2	13	61	24	113	5	3	.240/.278/.369

Comparables: Chance Sisco, John Ryan Murphy, Manuel Margot

Moreno, an infielder-turned-catcher and the youngest of the Jays' plethora of young backstops, broke onto the scene in 2018, continued to look great at the plate in 2019 as one of the younger players at Low-A Lansing, and was apparently a standout at the Jays' alternate site. After years of failing to deliver on would-be catchers of the future, it's a pleasant change of pace to have so many promising players at the position coming up through the system. With luck, one of them will loose the spectre of Russell Martin from its earthly tether, free to frame the stars in the night sky.

YEAR	TEAM	LVL	AGE	PA	DRC+	BABIP	BRR	FRAA	WARP
2018	BLU	ROK	18	101		.429			
2018	BLU	ROK	18	66		.312			
2019	LAN	LO-A	19	341	130	.282	0.4	C(54): 1.0	2.5
2021 FS	TOR	MLB	21	600	76	.277	0.0	C 0	0.6

Kevin Smith   SS

Born: 07/04/96   Age: 25   Bats: R   Throws: R
Height: 6'0"   Weight: 190   Origin: Round 4, 2017 Draft (#129 overall)

YEAR	TEAM	LVL	AGE	PA	R	2B	3B	HR	RBI	BB	K	SB	CS	AVG/OBP/SLG
2018	LAN	LO-A	21	204	36	23	4	7	44	17	33	12	1	.355/.407/.639
2018	DUN	HI-A	21	371	57	8	2	18	49	23	88	17	5	.274/.332/.468
2019	NH	AA	22	468	49	22	2	19	61	29	151	11	6	.209/.263/.402
2021 FS	TOR	MLB	24	600	57	23	2	20	67	33	205	9	4	.204/.254/.362

Comparables: Junior Lake, Orlando Calixte, Brad Harman

The major area of concern for Smith, a solid-but-not-stunning infield defender, is the leap in his strikeout rate—and the attendant decrease in his on-base ability—that he experienced after moving up to Double-A in 2019. Smith is a known swing-changer, having made adjustments in the offseason prior to his 2018 breakout; the next adjustment will have to be made while facing better pitchers.

YEAR	TEAM	LVL	AGE	PA	DRC+	BABIP	BRR	FRAA	WARP
2018	LAN	LO-A	21	204	189	.397	3.1	SS(24): 1.7, 3B(21): 0.7	3.2
2018	DUN	HI-A	21	371	125	.319	4.6	SS(63): 6.9, 2B(13): 1.0, 3B(6): -0.2	3.0
2019	NH	AA	22	468	91	.269	1.4	SS(87): 0.4, 3B(18): -1.1, 2B(5): -0.9	1.5
2021 FS	TOR	MLB	24	600	65	.281	0.6	SS 3, 3B 0	-0.7

Anthony Castro   RHP

Born: 04/13/95   Age: 26   Bats: R   Throws: R
Height: 6'2"   Weight: 182   Origin: International Free Agent, 2011

YEAR	TEAM	LVL	AGE	W	L	SV	G	GS	IP	H	HR	BB/9	K/9	K	GB%	BABIP
2018	LAK	HI-A	23	9	4	0	22	20	116²	112	8	3.3	7.8	101	48.7%	.310
2018	ERI	AA	23	0	0	0	3	3	10	8	1	10.8	3.6	4	50.0%	.226
2019	ERI	AA	24	5	3	1	27	18	102¹	75	9	5.7	10.2	116	43.4%	.274
2020	DET	MLB	25	0	0	0	1	0	1	1	1	9.0	9.0	1	0.0%	.000
2021 FS	TOR	MLB	26	2	3	0	57	0	50	48	8	5.2	8.4	46	40.8%	.288

Comparables: Bruce Billings, Sterling Sharp, Chris Stratton

It took eight years of bush-league buses to get the svelte Castro a single major-league inning last year. He's spent most of his career as a fill-in, moving from rotation to bullpen based on the status of other, more vaunted prospects, but his role has finally stabilized into middle relief. He'll likely begin 2021 in Triple-A after being claimed off waivers by the Blue Jays, but shouldn't have to wait another eight years for his second inning.

YEAR	TEAM	LVL	AGE	WHIP	ERA	DRA-	WARP	MPH	FB%	WHF	CSP
2018	LAK	HI-A	23	1.33	2.93	85	1.6				
2018	ERI	AA	23	2.00	8.10	100	0.1				
2019	ERI	AA	24	1.37	4.40	98	0.2				
2020	DET	MLB	25	2.00	18.00	112	0.0	93.1	58.8%	37.5%	
2021 FS	TOR	MLB	26	1.55	5.31	116	-0.2	93.1	58.8%	37.5%	40.1%

Ryan Feierabend   LHP

Born: 08/22/85   Age: 35   Bats: L   Throws: L
Height: 6'3"   Weight: 225   Origin: Round 3, 2003 Draft (#86 overall)

YEAR	TEAM	LVL	AGE	W	L	SV	G	GS	IP	H	HR	BB/9	K/9	K	GB%	BABIP
2018	KT	KBO	32	8	8	0	27	26	163^1	186	24	2.0	7.1	141		
2019	BUF	AAA	33	6	5	0	14	12	68^1	77	19	2.8	7.0	53	37.4%	.287
2019	TOR	MLB	33	0	1	0	2	1	5^2	11	2	1.6	6.4	4	41.7%	.409
2020	UNI	CPBL	34	2	3	0	11	10	57	67	5	3.2	8.7	55		
2021 FS	TOR	MLB	35	2	3	0	57	0	50	53	9	3.2	6.7	37	37.9%	.292

Comparables: Austin Bibens-Dirkx, Steven Wright, Chris Rusin

It's always fun to have a knuckleballer around, and the Lions enjoyed adding Feierabend to their squad prior to the 2020 season. His major league career split itself into three spread-out parts–2006-2008 with the Mariners, 2014 with the Rangers, and 2019 with the Blue Jays–but you could argue that the most important phase of his career was his four-year stay in the KBO, when the knuckler became an integral part of his pitching repertoire for the first time. Feierabend was a reliable member of the Lions' rotation from April to June while the team as a whole was struggling, but his stay with the team was short; his last game with the team was June 27th, as he returned home to be closer to family during the pandemic.

YEAR	TEAM	LVL	AGE	WHIP	ERA	DRA-	WARP	MPH	FB%	WHF	CSP
2018	KT	KBO	32	1.54	4.30						
2019	BUF	AAA	33	1.43	5.53	119	0.6				
2019	TOR	MLB	33	2.12	11.12	130	0.0	87.1	23.1%	23.3%	
2020	UNI	CPBL	34	1.53	4.74						
2021 FS	TOR	MLB	35	1.43	4.96	114	-0.2	87.1	23.1%	23.3%	23.5%

Ken Giles RHP

Born: 09/20/90   Age: 30   Bats: R   Throws: R
Height: 6'3"   Weight: 210   Origin: Round 7, 2011 Draft (#241 overall)

YEAR	TEAM	LVL	AGE	W	L	SV	G	GS	IP	H	HR	BB/9	K/9	K	GB%	BABIP
2018	FRE	AAA	27	0	0	0	6	0	5^1	9	0	3.4	13.5	8	41.2%	.529
2018	HOU	MLB	27	0	2	12	34	0	30^2	36	2	0.9	9.1	31	36.8%	.366
2018	TOR	MLB	27	0	1	14	21	0	19^2	18	4	1.8	10.1	22	51.8%	.275
2019	TOR	MLB	28	2	3	23	53	0	53	36	5	2.9	14.1	83	38.9%	.301
2020	TOR	MLB	29	0	0	1	4	0	3^2	4	2	9.8	14.7	6	44.4%	.286
2021 FS	TOR	MLB	30	3	2	0	57	0	50	39	6	3.2	11.9	65	40.4%	.291
2021 DC	TOR	MLB	30	2	2	0	52	0	45	35	6	3.2	11.9	59	40.4%	.291

Comparables: Cody Allen, Chris Devenski, Chad Green

Having Giles anchoring the back end of the Jays bullpen was supposed to be one of their strengths. Losing him for essentially the entire season was a disaster scenario. But that's exactly what happened: Giles made two appearances in July before getting injured. He made two more in September, both of which were so poor as to clearly indicate that something was still wrong. The Jays were able to survive the loss of their best reliever, but with Tommy John surgery and free agency on his horizon, we may have seen the last of him as a Blue Jay.

YEAR	TEAM	LVL	AGE	WHIP	ERA	DRA-	WARP	MPH	FB%	WHF	CSP
2018	FRE	AAA	27	2.06	8.44	26	0.2				
2018	HOU	MLB	27	1.27	4.99	76	0.5	98.9	57.8%	30.7%	
2018	TOR	MLB	27	1.12	4.12	71	0.4	98.9	61.3%	30.8%	
2019	TOR	MLB	28	1.00	1.87	53	1.6	98.9	50.7%	40.0%	
2020	TOR	MLB	29	2.18	9.82	82	0.1	96.2	38.5%	54.5%	
2021 FS	TOR	MLB	30	1.15	3.03	73	1.0	98.7	52.3%	38.4%	45.9%
2021 DC	TOR	MLB	30	1.15	3.03	73	0.9	98.7	52.3%	38.4%	45.9%

Alek Manoah   RHP

Born: 01/09/98   Age: 23   Bats: R   Throws: R
Height: 6'6"   Weight: 260   Origin: Round 1, 2019 Draft (#11 overall)

YEAR	TEAM	LVL	AGE	W	L	SV	G	GS	IP	H	HR	BB/9	K/9	K	GB%	BABIP
2019	VAN	SS	21	0	1	0	6	6	17	13	1	2.6	14.3	27	35.3%	.364
2021 FS	TOR	MLB	23	2	3	0	57	0	50	46	8	4.9	9.1	50	34.7%	.286

Comparables: Mitch Keller, Humberto Mejía, David Peterson

It got lost in the news with everything else going on, but this past spring, while excavating near the Devonian Fossil Gorge in Iowa, two undergraduate paleontology students accidentally unearthed a completely unexpected find: the first recorded evidence of a scouting report, etched into stone tablets. It read: "If he develops his changeup, he could be a third starter, but if not, with his fastball and slider, the floor is a late-inning reliever." Historians have long assumed that mankind passed this down from generation to generation by oral tradition since prehistoric times, but this was the first physical evidence confirming the theory. A team is prepared to return to the site next year to seek the ultimate missing link: the fabled 65-grade tool.

YEAR	TEAM	LVL	AGE	WHIP	ERA	DRA-	WARP	MPH	FB%	WHF	CSP
2019	VAN	SS	21	1.06	2.65	64	0.4				
2021 FS	TOR	MLB	23	1.47	4.85	114	-0.1				

Patrick Murphy   RHP

Born: 06/10/95   Age: 26   Bats: R   Throws: R
Height: 6'5"   Weight: 235   Origin: Round 3, 2013 Draft (#83 overall)

YEAR	TEAM	LVL	AGE	W	L	SV	G	GS	IP	H	HR	BB/9	K/9	K	GB%	BABIP
2018	DUN	HI-A	23	10	5	0	26	26	146²	126	5	3.1	8.3	135	57.5%	.299
2018	NH	AA	23	0	0	0	1	1	6	4	0	4.5	9.0	6	50.0%	.267
2019	NH	AA	24	4	7	0	18	18	84	75	7	2.9	9.2	86	51.6%	.286
2020	TOR	MLB	25	0	0	0	4	0	6	6	0	3.0	7.5	5	50.0%	.333
2021 FS	TOR	MLB	26	2	2	0	57	0	50	48	7	4.2	7.8	43	47.7%	.285
2021 DC	TOR	MLB	26	1	1	0	22	0	36	34	5	4.2	7.8	31	47.7%	.285

Comparables: Jimmy Lambert, Sterling Sharp, Sandy Baez

It's been a long, winding road for Murphy: injuries, a minor-league umpire telling him his delivery was illegal, more injuries after that. In 2020, though, he finally made it to the major leagues, called up from the alternate site in September, and acquitted himself very well over six scant innings. He has all the parts to serve as a bullpen arm, and the experience to appreciate the role.

YEAR	TEAM	LVL	AGE	WHIP	ERA	DRA-	WARP	MPH	FB%	WHF	CSP
2018	DUN	HI-A	23	1.20	2.64	110	0.0				
2018	NH	AA	23	1.17	3.00	50	0.2				
2019	NH	AA	24	1.21	4.71	91	0.5				
2020	TOR	MLB	25	1.33	1.50	90	0.1	98.1	59.6%	20.8%	
2021 FS	TOR	MLB	26	1.43	4.50	103	0.2	98.1	59.6%	20.8%	49.3%
2021 DC	TOR	MLB	26	1.43	4.50	103	0.1	98.1	59.6%	20.8%	49.3%

Joel Payamps RHP

Born: 04/07/94   Age: 27   Bats: R   Throws: R
Height: 6'2"   Weight: 225   Origin: International Free Agent, 2010

YEAR	TEAM	LVL	AGE	W	L	SV	G	GS	IP	H	HR	BB/9	K/9	K	GB%	BABIP
2018	JXN	AA	24	9	4	0	25	10	90	70	5	1.7	9.6	96	43.6%	.289
2018	RNO	AAA	24	0	4	0	6	5	26¹	35	5	3.4	8.9	26	31.8%	.366
2019	JXN	AA	25	3	4	0	7	7	40²	40	2	0.4	8.6	39	47.9%	.325
2019	RNO	AAA	25	2	2	0	8	8	38	41	6	3.8	7.1	30	41.7%	.312
2019	ARI	MLB	25	0	0	0	2	0	4	4	0	6.8	6.8	3	9.1%	.400
2020	ARI	MLB	26	0	0	0	2	0	3	2	0	9.0	6.0	2	12.5%	.250
2021 FS	TOR	MLB	27	2	3	0	57	0	50	50	8	3.8	7.9	44	39.0%	.293
2021 DC	TOR	MLB	27	0	0	0	18	0	18	18	3	3.8	7.9	16	39.0%	.293

Comparables: Keury Mella, Adrian Houser, Erick Fedde

Payamps got another miniscule audition for the Diamondbacks in 2020. And, just as in the season prior, he didn't do a lot with it. The good news is that his velo jumped as a pure reliever and that just might provide him a lengthier opportunity in 2021.

YEAR	TEAM	LVL	AGE	WHIP	ERA	DRA-	WARP	MPH	FB%	WHF	CSP
2018	JXN	AA	24	0.97	2.90	68	2.1				
2018	RNO	AAA	24	1.71	7.18	186	-0.9				
2019	JXN	AA	25	1.03	2.88	77	0.6				
2019	RNO	AAA	25	1.50	4.97	91	0.8				
2019	ARI	MLB	25	1.75	4.50	116	0.0	95.0	59.1%	22.7%	
2020	ARI	MLB	26	1.67	3.00	134	0.0	95.6	62.7%	23.5%	
2021 FS	TOR	MLB	27	1.43	4.73	111	-0.1	95.4	61.2%	23.2%	46.6%
2021 DC	TOR	MLB	27	1.43	4.73	111	0.0	95.4	61.2%	23.2%	46.6%

Trent Thornton   RHP

Born: 09/30/93   Age: 27   Bats: R   Throws: R
Height: 6'0"   Weight: 195   Origin: Round 5, 2015 Draft (#139 overall)

YEAR	TEAM	LVL	AGE	W	L	SV	G	GS	IP	H	HR	BB/9	K/9	K	GB%	BABIP
2018	FRE	AAA	24	9	8	0	24	22	124¹	118	13	2.2	8.8	122	41.6%	.305
2019	TOR	MLB	25	6	9	0	32	29	154¹	156	24	3.6	8.7	149	32.9%	.302
2020	TOR	MLB	26	0	0	0	3	3	5²	15	0	4.8	9.5	6	29.2%	.625
2021 FS	TOR	MLB	27	2	3	0	57	0	50	49	9	3.3	8.5	47	35.1%	.289
2021 DC	TOR	MLB	27	4	2	0	26	3	43.3	43	8	3.3	8.5	41	35.1%	.289

Comparables: Jakob Junis, Walker Lockett, Chase De Jong

Thornton became the unlikely anchor of the woebegone 2019 Jays rotation, accruing the most innings of any pitcher on the team. But any hoped-for development in his sophomore 2020 season was not to be. "Loose bodies" in his elbow hampered his performance in the mere 5⅔ innings, in which he appeared and ended his season in mid-August, with an unclear timeline for return. It was a somber moment indeed in the clubhouse when the right-hander removed his spectacles and handed them to Andrew Kay, completing a ritual that all men must perform, though all dread.

YEAR	TEAM	LVL	AGE	WHIP	ERA	DRA-	WARP	MPH	FB%	WHF	CSP
2018	FRE	AAA	24	1.20	4.42	83	2.3				
2019	TOR	MLB	25	1.41	4.84	124	-0.6	94.6	62.6%	24.5%	
2020	TOR	MLB	26	3.18	11.12	101	0.0	93.6	63.4%	19.1%	
2021 FS	TOR	MLB	27	1.36	4.61	105	0.1	94.5	62.7%	24.2%	43.4%
2021 DC	TOR	MLB	27	1.36	4.61	105	0.2	94.5	62.7%	24.2%	43.4%

Simeon Woods Richardson   RHP

Born: 09/27/00   Age: 20   Bats: R   Throws: R
Height: 6'3"   Weight: 210   Origin: Round 2, 2018 Draft (#48 overall)

YEAR	TEAM	LVL	AGE	W	L	SV	G	GS	IP	H	HR	BB/9	K/9	K	GB%	BABIP
2018	MTS	ROK	17	1	0	1	5	2	11¹	9	0	3.2	11.9	15	50.0%	.321
2018	KNG	ROK	17	0	0	0	2	2	6	6	1	0.0	16.5	11	38.5%	.417
2019	COL	LO-A	18	3	8	0	20	20	78¹	78	5	2.0	11.1	97	49.5%	.358
2019	DUN	HI-A	18	3	2	0	6	6	28¹	18	1	2.2	9.2	29	33.8%	.246
2021 FS	TOR	MLB	20	2	2	0	57	0	50	43	7	3.3	8.8	48	41.6%	.274

Comparables: Noah Syndergaard, Kolby Allard, Julio Urías

Woods-Richardson, who came over to the Jays in the Marcus Stroman deal, has progressed rapidly through the Jays' system. He's been impressive not only with his ability on the mound—he struck out 29 against walking just seven in 28⅓ innings at high-A Dunedin—but with his maturity, carrying himself in a manner beyond his years even as one of the youngest players at every level he reaches. That bodes well for his ability to wring value out of the lost 2020 season; lacking traditional competition, the Toronto coaching staff at the alternate site focused on mechanical improvements and applying technology. In Woods-Richardson's case, this includes refining a changeup to go with his already excellent fastball and promising curve.

YEAR	TEAM	LVL	AGE	WHIP	ERA	DRA-	WARP	MPH	FB%	WHF	CSP
2018	MTS	ROK	17	1.15	0.00						
2018	KNG	ROK	17	1.00	4.50						
2019	COL	LO-A	18	1.21	4.25	103	0.1				
2019	DUN	HI-A	18	0.88	2.54	62	0.7				
2021 FS	TOR	MLB	20	1.25	3.59	91	0.5				

Kirby Yates RHP

Born: 03/25/87   Age: 34   Bats: L   Throws: R
Height: 5'10"   Weight: 205   Origin: Round 26, 2005 Draft (#798 overall)

YEAR	TEAM	LVL	AGE	W	L	SV	G	GS	IP	H	HR	BB/9	K/9	K	GB%	BABIP
2018	SD	MLB	31	5	3	12	65	0	63	41	6	2.4	12.9	90	43.2%	.263
2019	SD	MLB	32	0	5	41	60	0	60²	41	2	1.9	15.0	101	47.5%	.328
2020	SD	MLB	33	0	1	2	6	0	4¹	7	1	8.3	16.6	8	38.5%	.500
2021 FS	TOR	MLB	34	3	2	32	57	0	50	38	6	3.1	12.4	69	40.8%	.292
2021 DC	TOR	MLB	34	3	2	32	62	0	54	41	6	3.1	12.4	74	40.8%	.292

Comparables: Brad Brach, Blake Parker, Oliver Drake

After two stellar seasons as one of the best relievers in baseball, Yates had a walk year to forget. He threw four disastrous innings before having to undergo season-ending surgery to remove bone chips from his pitching elbow. The good news is that he should be ready for the spring. The bad news is that a reliever going into his age-34 season and coming off elbow surgery is probably not going to get the big free-agent contract he seemed slated to receive. That's a rough break for someone who has had to grind his way to this point.

YEAR	TEAM	LVL	AGE	WHIP	ERA	DRA-	WARP	MPH	FB%	WHF	CSP
2018	SD	MLB	31	0.92	2.14	42	2.2	95.3	58.3%	34.8%	
2019	SD	MLB	32	0.89	1.19	41	2.2	94.7	57.1%	34.6%	
2020	SD	MLB	33	2.54	12.46	81	0.1	94.5	64.4%	41.3%	
2021 FS	TOR	MLB	34	1.10	2.80	69	1.1	94.8	58.1%	35.3%	44.2%
2021 DC	TOR	MLB	34	1.10	2.80	69	1.2	94.8	58.1%	35.3%	44.2%

T.J. Zeuch RHP

Born: 08/01/95   Age: 25   Bats: R   Throws: R
Height: 6'7"   Weight: 245   Origin: Round 1, 2016 Draft (#21 overall)

YEAR	TEAM	LVL	AGE	W	L	SV	G	GS	IP	H	HR	BB/9	K/9	K	GB%	BABIP
2018	DUN	HI-A	22	3	3	0	6	6	36^1	34	4	2.2	5.9	24	61.4%	.275
2018	NH	AA	22	9	5	0	21	21	120	120	7	2.3	6.1	81	55.2%	.299
2019	DUN	HI-A	23	0	0	0	2	2	8^2	7	0	2.1	12.5	12	59.1%	.318
2019	BUF	AAA	23	4	3	0	13	13	78	70	6	3.7	4.5	39	57.8%	.256
2019	TOR	MLB	23	1	2	0	5	3	22^2	22	2	4.4	7.9	20	48.5%	.303
2020	TOR	MLB	24	1	0	0	3	1	11^1	9	1	3.2	2.4	3	62.5%	.205
2021 FS	TOR	MLB	25	2	3	0	57	0	50	51	7	3.7	6.1	33	53.2%	.284
2021 DC	TOR	MLB	25	5	3	0	40	4	52.3	54	7	3.7	6.1	35	53.2%	.284

Comparables: Andrew Miller, Elieser Hernandez, Brandon Woodruff

If you think of every baseball season as a jigsaw puzzle, Zeuch's three late-season appearances were blurry pieces of sky and ... leaves? grass? Maybe it's not sky, it's actually water. Still, blurry as they might have been, the puzzle's not complete without them, and it did turn out to be a nice picture when it got finished.

YEAR	TEAM	LVL	AGE	WHIP	ERA	DRA-	WARP	MPH	FB%	WHF	CSP
2018	DUN	HI-A	22	1.18	3.47	121	-0.2				
2018	NH	AA	22	1.26	3.08	85	1.9				
2019	DUN	HI-A	23	1.04	4.15	44	0.3				
2019	BUF	AAA	23	1.31	3.69	81	2.1				
2019	TOR	MLB	23	1.46	4.76	108	0.1	94.0	52.5%	23.0%	
2020	TOR	MLB	24	1.15	1.59	100	0.1	93.9	77.3%	15.2%	
2021 FS	TOR	MLB	25	1.45	4.79	108	0.0	94.0	62.6%	19.8%	41.3%
2021 DC	TOR	MLB	25	1.45	4.79	108	0.1	94.0	62.6%	19.8%	41.3%

Blue Jays Prospects

The State of the System:

There's still some potential impact talent at the top, but less depth than recent editions.

The Top Ten:

───────── ★ ★ ★ *2021 Top 101 Prospect* **#22** ★ ★ ★ ─────────

1 **Austin Martin** **SS** OFP: 60 ETA: 2022
Born: 03/23/99 Age: 22 Bats: R Throws: R Height: 6'0" Weight: 185
Origin: Round 1, 2020 Draft (#5 overall)

The Report: A Swiss Army knife, a jack of all trades, he's basically the Dos Equis guy minus the hyperbolic backstory. Heading into the 2020 college season it appeared to be a two-horse race for the first overall pick between Martin and the eventual selection Spencer Torkelson. The previous year had put Martin squarely on track for the top of the draft: He hit for more power, got on base at a nearly 50 percent clip, was aggressive on the basepaths, and played all over the field defensively. It actually made it difficult when scouting him, knowing he was playing in so many different spots in the field and in the order to accommodate his team that you had to wonder if he was being knee-capped from displaying his true potential.

His spring season started exceptionally well. He rarely swung and missed, let alone struck out. It's a bit of a throwback swing; he keeps his hands low and relaxed at load and allows his body to fire off in sequence a short stride to waist bend that creates natural loft on his swing plane. Bat speed, barrel control, pitch recognition, he's got it all. The funny part about his role at Vanderbilt is that it will likely continue with the Jays, who could plug him in alongside other players who lack the same versatility and athleticism.

Development Track: It remains entirely possible that with young stars already entrenched on the major league roster that Martin could be aggressively pushed to join them while a contention window opens. So long as he handles each level of pitching with nary a challenge, his only real area of focus to develop is wherever he ends up positionally. Maybe the Jays want to keep him flexible, in which case, it's a fluid exercise interdependent of what his best position might be, and how fast the fast-track becomes wholly reliant on how much he hits.

Variance: High. We think he's going to hit, but not unlike Royce Lewis, there are some moving parts to the swing that could be tough to break if there are any hiccups. Without the hit tool and at least average power numbers, he drops to a quality utilityman.

J.P. Breen's Fantasy Take: I'm obviously no scout, but the above description (and pre-draft scouting reports) make Martin sound like an early-career Anthony Rendon—a guy who could play across the infield, hitting .270-.290 with 20 homers and 15 steals. If the average becomes late-career Rendon or his speed allows him to steal 20-plus bases, we're talking a potential elite five-category fantasy producer. He's a top-20 dynasty prospect for me.

─────── ★ ★ ★ *2021 Top 101 Prospect* **#35** ★ ★ ★ ───────

2

Nate Pearson   RHP   OFP: 60   ETA: Debuted in 2020
Born: 08/20/96   Age: 24   Bats: R   Throws: R   Height: 6'6"   Weight: 250
Origin: Round 1, 2017 Draft (#28 overall)

The Report: Pearson is one of the hardest throwing starting pitchers in baseball, sitting in the upper-90s much of the time and touching triple-digits often; he once hit 104 in the Arizona Fall League Fall Stars Game. He pairs that fastball velocity with a vicious hard slider that is already plus and flashing plus-plus. There aren't many pitch combinations from a starter that good, and Pearson also brings a curveball and changeup as usable additional offerings. His command is decent, although he does sometimes need to dial the velocity back to reach it, and his mechanics are reasonably smooth given the quality of his stuff. Injuries have been a recurring theme for him, dating back to a screw inserted into his elbow in high school, and including a broken pitching arm he suffered when a hard comebacker hit him in 2018.

Development Track: Toronto called Pearson up literally on the exact day they could claw back a year of his service time in July. His stuff was a little less loud and his command a little worse than we expected, and then he ended up missing more than a month with elbow/flexor problems. He came back very late in the season in a relief role, and the velocity ticked back up again airing it out. That might just be where this all ends up, although it won't be for lack of talent.

Variance: High. He's only pitched in one full season (2019) without getting hurt.

J.P. Breen's Fantasy Take: Pearson remains an elite dynasty pitching prospect. He missed fewer bats than expected—particularly in the zone compared to the rest of the league—but it's hard to separate his diminished stuff from his injury troubles. While Pearson has considerable variance in terms of his ultimate role, he should be a top-end arm, whether that's in the rotation or the bullpen. What separates Pearson from someone like A.J. Puk is that Puk suffered a dreaded shoulder injury. Pearson remains a top-20 dynasty prospect and a top-150 overall dynasty player.

——— ★ ★ ★ *2021 Top 101 Prospect* **#41** ★ ★ ★ ———

Jordan Groshans SS   OFP: 60   ETA: 2022/2023

3 Born: 11/10/99 Age: 21 Bats: R Throws: R Height: 6'3" Weight: 205

Origin: Round 1, 2018 Draft (#12 overall)

The Report: Groshans was one of the early breakouts of the 2019 campaign. He showed off a plus hit/plus power combination with very high polish for a prep hitter less than a year out from the draft. Then he went down with a foot injury about a month in. After some stops and starts, he never did find his way back to the field. We saw enough to view him as a potential middle-of-the-order bat anyway. Defensively, he's currently a shortstop, but we think he probably profiles best at third base over the long haul.

Development Track: Groshans was at the alternate site last summer getting much-needed reps. It's not quite a substitute for in-game work, and he absolutely needs those reps after missing most of 2019, but he was healthy and getting good work in.

Variance: High. The foot issues are hopefully in the past, but we still need to see in-game production over a full campaign (or as close to it as we'll get in 2021).

J.P. Breen's Fantasy Take: Groshans's combination of hit and power reminds me of Alex Kirilloff from a couple of years ago, except Groshans has more speed and scouts feel more confident in his long-term power production. The foot injury is scary, no doubt, but the 21-year-old is one of the most well-rounded impact hitting prospects in the minors. He's a top-50 guy in all formats.

——— ★ ★ ★ *2021 Top 101 Prospect* **#101** ★ ★ ★ ———

Alejandro Kirk C   OFP: 55   ETA: Debuted in 2020

4 Born: 11/06/98 Age: 22 Bats: R Throws: R Height: 5'8" Weight: 265

Origin: International Free Agent, 2016

The Report: Kirk's future is all about his hit tool and on-base abilities. He has plus-plus bat-to-ball skills coming out of a compact, direct swing. He pairs that with an excellent plate approach and pitch recognition, and indeed he walked more than he struck out at every minor-league level. We have projected him to this point with the hit tool dragging along the power; he hits the ball hard but without much loft in his swing to get it in the air, with a line-drive oriented approach. If he can start hitting it in the air more, there's a chance some more game power shows up.

Defensively, he's getting there. If you like your catcher frames short and stout, Kirk is the epitome of that. His arm is above-average and his receiving is improving. It was a big vote of confidence in his glove to get playing time behind the plate this year, and we think he's likely to stay at the position.

Development Track: Kirk was called up and got a bit of playing time down the stretch, even making a start at DH in the playoffs. He looked just fine as a 21-year-old catcher with only 151 professional games and none above A-ball, smashing the ball around in a handful of at-bats. That the Blue Jays even felt comfortable bringing him up into the playoff picture with that little experience is an extremely positive sign.

Variance: Medium. We're pretty confident he'll hit some and be able to catch at least part-time, so he has a high floor, but he is a young catcher.

J.P. Breen's Fantasy Take: A couple of years ago, dynasty owners everywhere drooled over the prospect of Willians Astudillo getting regular big-league at-bats. Although it never happened, Kirk could be the next best thing. If he can hit .280 with 10 homers in a good lineup, Kirk could be a top-10 fantasy catcher. He has the bat to do that, too. Fun fact: Only Wilson Ramos hit .280-plus with double-digit home runs among catchers in 2019.

5   **Orelvis Martinez**   **SS**   OFP: 55   ETA: 2023
Born: 11/19/01   Age: 19   Bats: R   Throws: R   Height: 6'1"   Weight: 188
Origin: International Free Agent, 2018

The Report: Martinez received the highest bonus of the Jays' J2 class in 2018 and put on a strong debut in 2019 that had the organization buzzing about 2020. Well it didn't really happen for him of course, but the organization still values Martinez very highly. He came to instructs with more physical strength, which was scary given that he was already posting high exit velos as a 17-year-old. This may mean he moves off short sooner rather than later, but the bat will play regardless. The logical position is third base given his plus arm strength and good instincts, as well as his physical stature.

Development Track: 2020 was the year Martinez was set to make his full-season debut, and we will have to wait until this year to see how it looks against better arms. He will play all of 2021 at 19 years old, so age isn't a detriment currently. We need to see him against better sequencing and for further development defensively.

Variance: High, but lower than last year? He is still a teenage prospect who hasn't faced competition outside the complex. The physical gains at such a young age are a concern, as it could mean some loss in athleticism.

J.P. Breen's Fantasy Take: Martinez is a bit less exciting as a dynasty prospect at third base, but it's still potential above-average power with a solid average. He's comfortably a top-100 dynasty prospect. If the power production is loud in full-season ball, or if he carries an elite average, his dynasty ranking might take a step forward. The fact that he won't steal double-digit bases, though, limits his ultimate upside.

6   **Simeon Woods Richardson**   **RHP**   OFP: 55   ETA: Late 2021/Early 2022
Born: 09/27/00   Age: 20   Bats: R   Throws: R   Height: 6'3"   Weight: 210
Origin: Round 2, 2018 Draft (#48 overall)

The Report: Woods Richardson fired himself off draft boards in 2018 after a velocity bump had him touching the upper-90s. He settled into the low-90s as a pro starter, reaching back for more at times, but the fastball had good late life and despite an uptempo delivery with some effort, Woods Richardson showed excellent body control and repeatability of the mechanics. Thus, strike-throwing has never really been a problem. His out pitch has been a power 12-6, high spin breaker, although he has at times struggled to command it as well as the fastball. It has the most likely plus outcome in the arsenal though. Woods Richardson replicates his arm speed well on the change but the pitch has generally had inconsistent shape and results.

Development Track: Woods Richardson added a slider at the alternate site, rounding out a full four-pitch mix. The fastball velocity was still more in an average band, and the longer he goes without tapping into that extra gear, the more likely the fastball just is what it is. It's enough fastball to start, and he's had no issues getting A-ball hitters out. The upper minors in 2021 will be the last test for the profile.

Variance: Medium. Woods Richardson has never consistently found his draft year pop-up velocity in the pros. He's built a more well-rounded arsenal in the interim, but there might not be that late inning relief fallback without the mid-90s heat. As a starter it's more a collection of average -> above-average stuff which might limit the upside.

J.P. Breen's Fantasy Take: Woods Richardson's dynasty stock remains a bit higher than his current scouting reports justify. Dynasty owners remember his 2018 breakout and won't let it go. At this point, though, the right-hander looks more like a solid mid-rotation starter without impressive strikeout numbers. Maybe the secondary stuff can carry him to SP3 territory. For now, though, you can treat him a bit like, say, Dane Dunning.

7 **C.J. Van Eyk**   OFP: 50   ETA: 2023
Born: 09/15/98   Age: 22   Bats: R   Throws: R   Height: 6'1"   Weight: 198
Origin: Round 2, 2020 Draft (#42 overall)

The Report: At a baseball powerhouse like Florida State, you expect young players to contribute right away, and then watch further maturation happen right in front of you for two or three years. In the case of Van Eyk, you saw flashes of the potential but always waited for the big breakout that never quite came. He's very much the same pitcher now that he was as a freshman, utilizing a low-to-mid-90s fastball to go along with a hard breaking downer curveball. The strikeouts have never been an issue, it's the command that has been suspect. The delivery could use some tightening up, as it lacks consistency and is often the source of the command issues.

Development Track: Beyond what can be done to help repeat his delivery more regularly, the changeup is mostly a show-me pitch with some arm-side fade that is telegraphed with his arm action. Development of that third pitch would help quell some of the reliever risk fears. Additionally, there's room on the frame to add a few extra pounds which could not only help with an extra tick of velocity, but help some of the core delivery problems as well.

Variance: Medium. After watching essentially the same product for three years, we have to believe he mostly is who he is.

J.P. Breen's Fantasy Take: Potential back-end starters who have issues with both their command and their third pitch are absolutely not my jam. Van Eyk isn't a top-400 dynasty prospect and can be safely avoided in all but the most ludicrous of formats.

8   **Alek Manoah**   **RHP**   OFP: 50   ETA: 2023
Born: 01/09/98   Age: 23   Bats: R   Throws: R   Height: 6'6"   Weight: 260
Origin: Round 1, 2019 Draft (#11 overall)

The Report: Mostly used as a reliever in his first two years in college, it took a breakout summer at the Cape Cod League, followed by a monster draft year at West Virginia, to convince scouts Manoah was worth the first-round grade as a future starter. The lively fastball and wicked slider combo can be very tough pitches to handle as he attacks the zone early and then tries to get chases out of it. The changeup is still M.I.A. which would help alleviate some of the platoon issues he'd face in a major league rotation. However, the main concern regarding his days as a starter possibly being numbered are reports from camp that had his velocity down more in the low 90s.

Development Track: He's always had a notoriously bad body, listed at 260 pounds it isn't weight carried well, showing in his delivery. There's plenty of effort needed to generate the kinetic energy used to drive down the mound, so any further deterioration of his physique will negatively impact all parts of his game. 2020 was a weird year for pitchers though, so perhaps he bounces back with a more normal minor league season.

Variance: Very High. Things are going in the wrong direction for Manoah. He's young and there is still plenty of time to turn it around, but the relief risk has been there since college.

J.P. Breen's Fantasy Take: This might be the first pitching prospect to reportedly have their stuff regress in 2020. The relief risk, the body risk, and the disappointing camp reports all should have him tumbling out of our top-400 dynasty lists. No wonder folks in our experts leagues have been trying to float Manoah on the trade block.

9 **Gabriel Moreno** C   OFP: 50   ETA: 2022 or 2023
Born: 02/14/00 Age: 21 Bats: R Throws: R Height: 5'11" Weight: 160
Origin: International Free Agent, 2016

The Report: Moreno was sent to the Midwest League as a 19-year-old catcher and more than held his own. It's a hit-over-power profile at present with good bat control, but he already shows an ability to sting the ball despite minimal weight transfer, and he should grow into more strength on what is presently a relatively slight frame for a catcher. The profile is also bat-first as Moreno is inexperienced behind the plate and will need to work on his receiving. He will also need to show he can handle the rigors of a full catching workload up the ladder.

Development Track: Despite the need for extra catchers at any alternate site, Toronto didn't send Moreno to their alternate site in Rochester. I wouldn't read too much into his absence given the relatively stable Blue Jays catching situation and he did get instructs time. Still, that likely keeps him on a relatively conservative time table, with an Advanced-A assignment on tap for 2021 in all likelihood.

Variance: High. There's a fair bit of positive variance here. Moreno could improve enough defensively to where the above-average offensive projection makes him a good starter. He could add enough power that you live with fringy defense. But catchers are weird, and we aren't quite convinced he's a catcher yet.

J.P. Breen's Fantasy Take: Moreno is more interesting in real life than in fantasy baseball. Without monster power or a batting average that annually pushes .290, he doesn't profile as someone who could potentially be a top-10 fantasy catcher in the big leagues. Since that's the case, Moreno would have to be on the cusp of the majors to be worth rostering in most dynasty formats. More interesting low-level catching prospects exist for fantasy purposes, if that's your thing.

10 **T.J. Zeuch** RHP   OFP: 50   ETA: Debuted in 2019
Born: 08/01/95 Age: 25 Bats: R Throws: R Height: 6'7" Weight: 245
Origin: Round 1, 2016 Draft (#21 overall)

The Report: I said last year that Zeuch throws a "bushel of average or slightly-above pitches," and that's still what we've got here. Pitch Info has already picked up six distinct offerings—four-seam fastball, sinker, cutter, slider, changeup, and curveball—over his 34 MLB innings. The sinker is the best of them, and it's the above-average one, coming in mostly in the low-90s with quality movement and a good angle given his height. All of the offspeeds are fine, but there's no swing-and-miss pitch here, so there's way less upside than you'd think or hope for from a first-round pitcher. He has advanced pitchability and command.

Development Track: It's a bit surprising that Zeuch wasn't up earlier in the season. The Blue Jays called upon him in mid-September, and he had a couple nice long relief appearances. He got a start in the last week of the season and threw five shutout innings without registering a strikeout or walk. His stuff was pretty much the same as past reports.

Variance: Low. Zeuch is what he is.

J.P. Breen's Fantasy Take: Zeuch is useful enough as a real-life big leaguer, but he's not worth rostering in dynasty leagues. He walks too many guys and doesn't miss enough bats to be interesting.

The Prospects You Meet Outside The Top Ten

Prospects to dream on a little

Leonardo Jimenez   2B   Born: 05/17/01   Age: 20   Bats: R   Throws: R   Height: 5'11"   Weight: 160   Origin: International Free Agent, 2017

Signed out of Panama in 2017, Jimenez is one of the best defenders in the organization at SS. He has quality hands with a smooth easy arm that rates as above-average. Not a burner but he shows a quick first step and has the instincts one looks for at short. He hasn't shown much power in-game, but came to instructs with more physicality, including hitting a home run (which he has yet to do in an official game). The glove is the noteworthy item here, but with an improving offensive skill set he can become a hidden gem in the org.

Miguel Hiraldo   3B   Born: 09/05/00   Age: 20   Bats: R   Throws: R   Height: 5'11"   Weight: 170   Origin: International Free Agent, 2017

A bat-first infielder, Hiraldo has one of the more notable hit/power combo in the organization, which is what is going to have to carry him going forward. The bat is loud but can be exploited as he is quite pull happy and can loop his hands while loading. But pitcher-beware: when Hiraldo connects it often goes a long way. Hiraldo has filled out more now and has always struggled with his lateral range, so he won't be a shortstop for long and projects as a keystone player.

Eric Pardinho   RHP   Born: 01/05/01   Age: 20   Bats: R   Throws: R   Height: 5'10"   Weight: 155   Origin: International Free Agent, 2017

Pardinho starred for Team Brazil in the 2016 WBC qualifiers as a 15-year-old, and that made him pretty famous for a teenage prospect. He signed for $1.4 million the following summer, and at the beginning of his pro career he was extremely advanced and on the fringes of Top 101 prospect contention; he didn't actually make it owing to his limited projection. Unfortunately, he started dealing with elbow problems in 2019 and had Tommy John surgery last spring. At his best he's got a fastball he can command in the low-to-mid-90s and a plus curve, but we need to see him throw a full season before we're going to be back in substantially.

MLB arms, but probably relievers

Jackson Rees **RHP**   Born: 07/30/94   Age: 26   Bats: R   Throws: R   Height: 6'4"   Weight: 210   Origin: Undrafted Free Agent, 2018

Rees struggled with effectiveness and injuries as an amateur, signing to no fanfare for $1K as an UDFA. I mentioned him as an interesting pop-up arm in 2019 spring training, and he popped up for sure. He finished the year with over 12 Ks per 9, a 0.73 ERA, and earned a spot in the Arizona Fall League. Toronto, recognizing his size, moved his arm slot higher and had him pitching in shorter stints out of the bullpen, which increased his velocity. He is now 95-96 with hard cut and deception, as well as featuring a plus slider that has quality vertical depth. At 26, and turning 27 in July, Rees will be on the fastrack as long as he keeps getting outs.

MLB bats, but less upside than you'd like

Kevin Smith **SS**   Born: 07/04/96   Age: 25   Bats: R   Throws: R   Height: 6'0"   Weight: 190   Origin: Round 4, 2017 Draft (#129 overall)

Smith dropped from the 101 long list in 2019, to barely on the Jays' list in 2020. A swing change intended to boost Smith's power instead sapped his whole stat line. He's been working his way back to the old swing in 2020, but fits better as a good bench infielder nowadays.

Top Talents 25 and Under (as of 4/1/2021):

1. Vladimir Guerrero Jr., 1B/3B
2. Bo Bichette, SS
3. Austin Martin, IF
4. Nate Pearson, RHP
5. Cavan Biggio, 2B/3B/OF
6. Jordan Groshans, SS
7. Danny Jansen, C
8. Alejandro Kirk, C
9. Orelvis Martinez, IF
10. CJ Van Eyk, RHP

Yeah, we know Vladdy hasn't actually gotten close to the 8 hit/8 power projection we put on him yet. He's played two MLB seasons, posted a better-than-average DRC+ in both, and he hasn't even turned 22 yet. Give it time.

Bo Bichette has also played two MLB seasons, has also posted a better-than-average DRC+ in both of his MLB seasons, and instead of bouncing between the corners has played an acceptable shortstop. He's a star too, even if he could do with trying to yank it to Mars a few less times a week, and he's closing the gap with Guerrero for the best son of a '90s star in the system.

Incredibly, those two actually have additional competition. Cavan Biggio, who was a much lesser prospect than either, has also posted a better than-average DRC+ in both of his MLB seasons—actually, the best offensive output of any of the three. He's a versatile defender who has some pop and walks a lot, and that's carried his production thus far.

Danny Jansen, our 2019 No. 89 prospect, only hit .183 in 2020, but that belies a 108 DRC+. He's not a star, and as far as I know he's not related to anyone I watched play baseball when I was a kid. But he's looking like a decent starting catching, even if the hit tool is lacking some, and there aren't a lot of those floating around.

Part 3: Featured Articles

Blue Jays All-Time Top 10 Players

by Steven Goldman

POSITION PLAYERS

JOHN OLERUD, 1B (1989–1996)

The starting first baseman for the Blue Jays' two World Series winners, in 1992 and 1993, Olerud had one of the great seasons in team history in the latter year. Hitting .400 as late as August 2, he won the batting title with a .363 average, led the American League with a 186 OPS+, and led the majors with 54 doubles and a .473 on-base percentage. In the previous 30 years, the only player to post a higher on-base percentage in either league had been Wade Boggs, with a .476 mark in 1988. After that big season, Cito Gaston pushed Olerud to become a pull hitter, a decision which damaged both the player and the team. Drafted by Toronto in 1989's third round, Olerud went directly from Washington State University, where he had suffered a brain aneurysm that prompted him to always wear a helmet in the field, to the major leagues. Even after he was gone, Gaston complained that he didn't smile enough.

CARLOS DELGADO, 1B (1993–2004)

The Blue Jays' all-time leader in plate appearances (6,018), home runs (336), doubles (343), walks (827), intentional walks (128), runs scored (889), RBI (1,058), extra-base hits (690), and total bases (2,786). Delgado was a minor league catcher who didn't settle in at first base until his age-25 season. Then, from age 26 to 31, he hit .295/.413/.585 (155 OPS+) while averaging 40 home runs, 40 doubles, 101 walks, 107 runs scored, 124 RBI, and 324 total bases per season, and winning three Silver Sluggers in those six seasons at a position that was stacked with sluggers league-wide. On the final Thursday of his age-31 season, Delgado became just the 13th player since 1900—as well as the second-oldest and still the only Blue Jay—to hit four home runs in a single game. He remains the only player ever to hit four home runs in a game in which he only came to the plate four times. Born and raised in Aguadilla, Puerto Rico, Delgado was active in protesting the U.S. Navy's use of Vieques as a live-weapons testing site in the early 2000s and, in 2004, remained in the dugout during the playing of "God Bless America" in protest of the Iraq War.

ROBERTO ALOMAR, 2B (1991–1995)

The first (and technically only) player inducted into the National Baseball Hall of Fame as a Blue Jay, Alomar was acquired by the Jays in a blockbuster four-player trade with the Padres in December 1990 that sent first baseman Fred McGriff and franchise icon Tony Fernández (see below) to the Padres for Alomar and outfielder Joe Carter. Already an All-Star in 1990 with San Diego—where his father, Sandy, was a coach—Alomar blossomed into a superstar in Toronto, making the All-Star team and winning the Gold Glove in all five of his seasons with the team (and starting at second base in four of those five All-Star Games), adding a Silver Slugger in 1992, and finishing sixth in the AL MVP voting every year from 1991 to 1993. Alomar hit .307/.382/.451 (123 OPS+) as a Blue Jay while averaging 41 stolen bases (at an 82 percent success rate) and seven triples per season. He hit .373/435/.492 in 133 postseason plate appearances for the team, winning the MVP award of the 1992 American League Championship Series, and hitting .480 in the 1993 World Series. Despite spending just five seasons with the team, he is second all-time in franchise history with 206 stolen bases.

TONY FERNÁNDEZ, SS (1983–1990, 1993, 1998–1999, 2001)

A contact-hitting switch-hitter whose loose-handed batting style recalled that of Hall of Famer Rod Carew, Fernández was a quietly outstanding all-around player from the baseball hotbed of San Pedro de Macoris in the Dominican Republic. In his initial stint with the Blue Jays, Fernández won four Gold Gloves at shortstop, made three All-Star teams, and was typically good for a .290 batting average, 20-odd stolen bases, and a good number of triples. In 1990, he led the majors with 17 three-baggers. In 1987, he hit .322. Traded away in the deal for Alomar, Fernández was reacquired in June 1993 and hit .326 with a .400 on-base percentage as the team's starting shortstop in that October's championship run. After returning, again, as a free agent, he hit .328/.427/.449 in 1999, batting .400 as late as June 28, and made his fourth All-Star team as a Blue Jay at the age of 37, this time as a third baseman. Returning to the team as a free agent one last time, in June 2001, he finished his career by coming off the bench and hitting .305 for the team for which he remains the all-time leader in games (1,450), hits (1,583), and triples (72). In total, Fernández hit .297/.353/.412 across his four stints with the Jays during the regular season, and .333/.381/.402 in 98 postseason plate appearances for Toronto.

LLOYD MOSEBY, OF (1980–1989)

Barfield, Bell, and center fielder Lloyd Moseby were widely regarded as the best outfield in baseball in the mid-1980s, a title they ultimately ceded to the Pirates' Barry Bonds-Andy Van Slyke-Bobby Bonilla triumvirate in 1988. According to convention, Moseby was the speed in the middle of that slugger sandwich, and he is still the Jays' all-time leader in stolen bases (255) and ranks second in franchise history in triples with 60. From 1983 to 1987, Moseby hit .277/.355/.456 (117 OPS+) while averaging 20 homers, 35 stolen bases (at a 78 percent success rate), and eight triples per season, winning the Silver Slugger in 1983, leading the league with 15 triples in 1984, and making his only All-Star team in 1986. In his final act with Toronto, Moseby, who had been the second-overall pick in the 1978 draft, was the team's most productive hitter in the 1989 ALCS against the A's, going 5-for-16 (.313) with a home run and five walks, albeit in a losing effort. Injuries brought a premature close to Moseby's peak period, and his major league career ended when he was just 31.

JESSE BARFIELD, OF (1981–1989)

Jesse Barfield was the best player on the first Blue Jays team to reach the postseason. In 1985, Barfield, an outstanding right fielder with a rocket arm, hit .289/.369/.536 (141 OPS+) with 27 home runs, 22 stolen bases, and nine triples. The next year, he replicated the batting average and on-base percentage but goosed the homer total to a major-league-leading 40, made his first All-Star team, won the Silver Slugger and the Gold Glove, and finished fifth in the AL MVP voting. He was never that good again and would be flipped to the Yankees for an overworked young left-hander named Al Leiter a month into the 1989 season, but Barfield did win another Gold Glove and hit 28 homers in 1987. His throwing arm is still mentioned with reverence nearly 30 years after the end of his playing career—he led the AL in assists from right field six times and his career total of 154 ranks 16th on the career list.

GEORGE BELL, OF (1981, 1983–1990)

Just because George Bell was overrated doesn't mean he wasn't good. He was a steal, drafted away from the Phillies in the 1980 Rule 5 draft at a time when the rules allowed the occasional quality player to slip through. Primarily a left fielder in Toronto, Bell was brutal in the field, and he didn't have much interest in drawing walks, but he could hit. From 1984 to 1989, Bell put up a .292/.332/.503 line while averaging 29 homers, 104 RBI, and just 73 strikeouts per year. Bell only made one All-Star team during that six-year stretch, but he won three Silver Sluggers and finished in the top eight in the MVP voting four times, winning the award in 1987 for a season in which he hit 47 home runs, scored 111 times, drove in a league-leading 134 runs, and led the majors in that rabbit-ball season with 369 total bases. The next year, he hit a record three home runs on Opening Day, giving him 50 over his previous 157 games. He was an All-Star again in 1990, but his bat went cold in the second half of that year and the Jays let him leave as a free agent after the season.

VERNON WELLS, OF (1999–2010)

Selected by the Blue Jays out of his Arlington, Texas high school with the fifth-overall pick in the 1997 draft, Wells was in the majors just two years later but didn't establish himself as the Jays' everyday centerfielder until his age-23 season in 2002. Wells had a proper breakout the next year, leading the majors with 215 hits and the AL with 49 doubles and 373 total bases to go with 33 home runs, 118 runs scored, 117 RBI, and a .317 average. An All-Star and Silver Slugger that year, he won the Gold Glove the next three and largely replicated that 2003 breakout in 2006 by hitting .303/.357/.542 with 32 homers and 106 RBI, adding award-worthy play in center and 17 stolen bases (at an 81 percent success rate). That was Wells' age-27 season, and, after dragging their feet for several years, the Jays finally decided to lock him up long term that December, signing him to a seven-year, $126 million extension. He was almost immediately undone by injuries. A torn labrum in his right shoulder torpedoed his hitting in 2007; his fielding collapsed thereafter amid hamstring and wrist injuries. Wells hit 31 home runs and made another All-Star team in 2010, but by then the Jays were desperate to unload his albatross of a contract. They seized on that strong showing to flip him and all but $5 million of the $86 million left on his contract to the Angels for catcher Mike Napoli and outfielder Juan Rivera, both of whom were gone before the 2011 trading deadline. Wells spent parts of a dozen years in Toronto and ranks second in franchise history in plate appearances (5,963), hits (1,529), doubles (339), RBI (813), extra-base hits (592), and total bases (2,597).

JOSÉ BAUTISTA, OF (2008–2017)

When the Blue Jays acquired Bautista from the Pirates straight-up for catcher Robinzon Díaz in August 2008, he was a marginally useful third baseman/utility player who would draw some walks and hit 15 homers a year. He was also changing teams for the sixth time in five years. Through the first five months of the 2009 season, he hit three home runs. That September, acting on first-base coach Dwayne Murphy's advice to start his swing earlier, Bautista hit 10. In 2010, his seventh major-league season, he hit 54, all but one pulled to the left side of dead center. Bautista's was one of the most shocking breakout performances in the game's history, but it was no fluke. From 2010 to 2015, a six-year span covering his age-29 to -34 seasons, Joey Bats hit .268/.390/.555, averaging 45 home runs and 113 walks per 162 games. He made the All-Star Game all six of those years, starting four of them in right field, won three Silver Sluggers, and finished in the top eight in the AL MVP voting four times. In the last of those seasons, the Jays snapped a 20-year playoff drought. Bautista hit .293/.408/.659 in 49 plate appearances in that postseason, including a series-winning, three-run home run in the seventh inning of Game 5 of the Division Series against the Rangers punctuated by the greatest bat flip in major-league history. Injuries and age wore him down from there, but Bautista still ranks second in franchise history in home runs (288), walks (803), and runs scored (790).

EDWIN ENCARNACIÓN, DH/1B (2009–2016)

The Blue Jays rescued Encarnación from his Sisyphean battles with third base in Cincinnati, moved him across the diamond and to designated hitter and just let him hit. From 2012 to 2016, Encarnación hit .272/.367/.544 (146 OPS+) averaging 39 home runs, 110 RBI, and fewer than 100 strikeouts per year, making three All-Star teams and picking up MVP votes in four of those five seasons. Over those five years, only Chris Davis hit more home runs (edging Encarnación 197 to 193 while Encarnación struck out fewer than half as many times as Davis) and only Miguel Cabrera drove in more runs (again accompanied by more strikeouts). By the end of that run, Encarnación was third in franchise history in home runs with 239. Not included in that count was the most memorable: His 11th inning walkoff to win the 2016 Wild Card Game against the Orioles. On April 27, 2014, Encarnación and Bautista were part of a Blue Jays starting lineup that included six Dominican-born players, a major-league record and cause for celebration for the players involved.

PITCHERS

JIM CLANCY, RHP (1977–1988)

Of all the players selected in the November 1976 expansion draft, only catcher Ernie Whitt spent more time in a Blue Jays uniform than 6-foot-4 Chicago native Jim Clancy, who was selected out of the Rangers' system with the sixth overall pick in that draft. Clancy made his major league debut in July of the Jays' inaugural season and, save for injury-shortened campaigns in 1979 and 1985, was a workhorse in the Toronto rotation for the next 11 and a half years. More stalwart than star, he did make the All-Star team in 1982, a season in which he posted a 121 ERA+ in 266 2/3 innings and a major-league leading 40 starts. On the whole, Clancy was a league-average starter for the Jays, but he filled that role for 12 years and thus ranks second in franchise history in innings (2,204 2/3), games started (345), and complete games (73), and third in shutouts (11) and wins (128).

DAVE STIEB, RHP (1979–1992, 1998)

Though deserved run average suggests we have overcorrected in our retroactive elevation of Stieb, it's true that he was greatly underappreciated during his career. The Blue Jays' all-time leader in innings (2,873), starts (439), complete games (103), shutouts (30), strikeouts (1,658) and wins (175), Stieb was also the best pitcher in baseball in the window between Steve Carlton's two early-'80s Cy Youngs and the emergence of Dwight Gooden and Roger Clemens in the middle of the decade. In the six years from 1980 to 1985, Stieb made five All-Star teams and finished in the top seven in the Cy Young voting three times. In the last four years of that stretch, he posted a 2.91 ERA (148 ERA+) while averaging 275 innings per season. In 1982, he led the AL in innings (288 1/3) and shutouts (5) and the majors in complete games (19). In '84, he led the majors in innings (267) and ERA+ (146). In 1985, he led the AL in ERA (2.48) and ERA+ (171) and started three games in that year's ALCS, dominating in the Game 1, but with diminishing returns thereafter. Drafted as an outfielder, Stieb converted to pitching in his first professional season in 1978 and was in the Jays' rotation the next year. Despite that late conversion, the bitter irony of Stieb's career is that he was great before the Blue Jays were good, merely good after the team rose to contention, and injured during their championship run in 1992. Still, he did make two more All-Star teams after that early period of dominance and finished fifth in the Cy Young voting in 1990 with a 140 ERA+ in 208 2/3 innings. Stieb authored the only no-hitter in Blue Jays history in 1990, but he is better remembered for the many near-misses that preceded it, including consecutive starts in 1988 in which he lost the no-no with one out to go and a near-perfect game against the Yankees in 1989 that was broken up by the 27th batter.

JIMMY KEY, LHP (1984–1992)

Along with the maturation of Jesse Barfield, the emergence of Henke, and a strong overall year from the bullpen, Key's move into the Blue Jays' rotation as a major-league sophomore in 1985 was a huge part of Toronto's 10-game improvement that season and thus their first-ever division championship and playoff berth. A slim, curveballing groundballer with impeccable control, Key posted a 3.00 ERA (141 ERA+) in 212 2/3 innings for the '85 Jays, making the All-Star team in his first season as a starter. Two years later, he defied the rabbit ball by leading the majors with a 2.76 ERA, 164 ERA+, and 1.06 WHIP over 261 innings, finishing second in the Cy Young voting to Roger Clemens. Elbow surgery and a torn rotator cuff interrupted two of his next three seasons and undermined his ability to induce grounders, but Key was an All-Star again in 1991 and posted a 0.75 ERA across 12 innings of work in the 1992 postseason, earning World Series wins in Game 4 (as a starter) and the decisive Game 6 (an inning and a third of relief on two-day's rest).

TOM HENKE, RHP (1985–1992)

On December 5, 1984, the Texas Rangers signed 37-year-old designated hitter Cliff Johnson, who had posted a 136 OPS+ over the previous two seasons for the Blue Jays. Under the rules of the day, that entitled the Jays to a compensation pick from the Rangers' organization. On January 24, they selected a 27-year-old righty reliever with control problems who had posted a 6.35 ERA the year before and wore large, wire-rimmed glasses that made him look like an accountant. His name was Tom Henke, and, with the Blue Jays, he would almost instantly emerge as one of the most dominant closers of his era. Dubbed "the Terminator" as much for his milquetoast appearance as his legitimate ability to terminate games, in eight seasons with Toronto Henke would post a 2.48 ERA with a 1.03 WHIP, 10.3 strikeouts per nine innings, and a 3.88 strikeout-to-walk ratio. Among pitchers with at least 500 innings pitched between 1985 and 1992, Henke's 167 ERA+ was the best in baseball, and his WHIP and strikeout-to-walk ratio trailed only those of Hall of Famer Dennis Eckersley. In his final four years with Toronto, Henke got even tougher, shrinking his ERA to a miniscule 2.14 (187 ERA+). In the postseason, Henke strung together 12 straight scoreless appearances spanning 14 1/3 innings from his final outing in the 1985 ALCS through saves in Games 2 and 4 of the 1992 World Series. Toronto's all-time leader in saves, his 217 are nearly 100 more than those of runner-up Duane Ward.

DAVID WELLS, LHP (1987–1992, 1999–2000)

A second-round pick out of Don Larsen's high school in 1982, Wells first emerged in the Blue Jays' bullpen in 1987, then spent three years as a high-volume swing man from 1990 to 1992. In that initial Jays stint, Wells started 69 games, made 168 relief appearances, averaged 115 innings per season, recorded 13 saves, and posted a 108 ERA+, adding a 1.38 ERA in 13 innings of relief across three postseasons, including a hold in the decisive game of the 1992 World Series. He then left as a free agent to join a club that would let him start full time. In 1998, he was the ace of a Yankees team that has gone down as one of the best in major-league history. The following spring, the Jays reacquired Wells as the primary return for two-time defending Cy Young award winner Roger Clemens. Now 36, Wells led the AL in innings (231.2) and complete games (7) in 1999, then went 20-8 with a 123 ERA+ in 229 2/3 innings, including a major-league leading nine complete games, in 2000. For that performance, he made his third All-Star team, finished third in the Cy Young voting, and collected some down-ballot MVP votes. The following January, the Jays traded Wells in a six-player deal built around 29-year-old lefty Mike Sirotka. Sirotka arrived with a bum shoulder and never threw another competitive pitch as a professional.

JUAN GUZMÁN, RHP (1991–1998)

Dominican right-hander Juan Guzmán was the ace of the Blue Jays' back-to-back world champions in 1992 and 1993. The AL Rookie of the Year runner-up in 1991, Guzmán posted a 2.79 ERA (149 ERA+) in his first two big-league seasons, making his only All-Star team as a sophomore and going 3-0 with a 2.03 ERA in the 1992 postseason, with each of his four starts better than the last. In 1993, he set a career high with 221 innings and finished seventh in the Cy Young voting despite a more pedestrian 3.99 ERA. Similarly, he excelled in three of his four starts that postseason, posting a 2.88 ERA and suffering a hard-luck loss in Game 5 of the World Series. A falling strikeout rate and rising walk rate dropped him below average in the strike-shortened seasons of 1994 and 1995, but he rebounded to win the AL ERA title in 1993 with a 2.93 mark while also leading the league in ERA+ (171), WHIP (1.12), and strikeout-to-walk ratio (3.11). That was his last great season for the Jays, however, as walks, homers, and injuries got to him in 1997, and the Jays dealt him to Baltimore at the 1998 trading deadline.

PAT HENTGEN, RHP (1991–1999, 2004)

Detroit native Pat Hentgen succeeded Juan Guzmán as the Blue Jays' ace in the years surrounding the 1994 strike. An All-Star and sixth-place finisher in the Cy Young voting for the 1993 champions, from then through 1997 Hentgen made three All-Star teams and posted a 123 ERA+ while averaging 224 innings per season despite the time lost to the strike. In 1996 and '97, he led the majors in innings, topping 260 each year. He also led the AL in complete games (9) and shutouts (3) in 1997 and the majors in those categories (10 complete games, three shutouts) in 1996, the year he went 20-10 and edged out the Yankees' Andy Pettitte for the AL Cy Young award. The heavy workloads of the Cito Gaston years caught up to him thereafter.

ROGER CLEMENS, RHP (1997–1998)

When Clemens signed a three-year, $24.75 million contract with the Blue Jays in December 1996, Red Sox general manager Dan Duquette, citing the Rocket's diminishing innings totals from 1993 to 1995, said that the 34-year-old, three-time Cy Young award winner was in the twilight of his career. Whether or not that motivated Clemens with regard to his performance or his performance-enhancing drug use (Blue Jays strength and conditioning coach Brian McNamee testified in 2012 that he injected Clemens with steroids during the second half of the 1998 season, describing a scenario in which this appeared to be a routine procedure for the veteran ace), Clemens' dominance in his two seasons in Toronto stands as one of the all-time great servings of crow in the game's history. In arguably the greatest season in one of the greatest pitching careers in the game's history, Clemens, in 1997, led the majors with 264 innings, a 222 ERA+, 2.25 FIP, and 21 wins, and the American League with a 2.05 ERA, nine complete games, three shutouts, 292 strikeouts, and a 1.03 WHIP. In 1998, he again led the majors with 20 wins and the AL in ERA (2.65), ERA+ (174), FIP (2.65), and strikeouts (271 in 234 2/3 innings). Clemens won the AL Cy Young award both seasons, doing so unanimously in 1998, while also placing in the top 11 in the MVP voting both years. Then, just as pitchers and catchers were reporting to spring training in 1999, the Blue Jays traded him to the Yankees for the third-place finisher in the previous year's Cy Young voting, David Wells (see below), lefty reliever Graeme Lloyd, and second baseman Homer Bush. Clemens would pitch nine more years and win two more Cy Youngs but to date has been denied entry to the Hall of Fame.

ROY HALLADAY, RHP (1998–2009)

Drafted 17th overall out of his Colorado high school in 1995, Halladay debuted in the majors in 1998 and posted a 130 ERA+ in 163 1/3 innings over his first two seasons, but, in 1999 and 2000, he walked nearly as many men as he struck out and his ERA ballooned to 10.64 in the latter season. In an effort to reprogram him, the Blue Jays demoted him all the way down to A-ball to start 2001 and brought veteran pitching coach Mel Queen out of retirement to rebuild Halladay's mechanics and mental approach. It worked. Halladay returned to the majors that June and posted a 3.84 strikeout-to-walk ratio over 105 1/3 innings. The next year, he was an All-Star. In 2003, he was the American League's Cy Young award winner and led the majors with a 6.38 K/BB. Injuries interrupted in 2004 (shoulder soreness) and 2005 (broken leg via comebacker), but, from 2006 to 2009, he averaged 233 innings per year and finished in the top five in the Cy Young voting every year, including a second-place finish in 2008. A throwback in terms of workloads, Halladay, over his last seven seasons in Toronto, led the AL in complete games five times and the majors thrice, and the AL thrice and the majors once in shutouts. He also led the league in innings twice and the majors in strikeout-to-walk ratio three times. From 2001 to 2009, he posted a 3.13 ERA (145 ERA+) with a 4.08 strikeout-walk rate, averaged more than 200 innings per season despite missing time in three of those seasons, and made six All-Star teams, starting the game in 2009. Traded to the Phillies in December 2009 ahead of impending free agency (and his second Cy Young award), he ranks second in Blue Jays history in wins (148), strikeouts (1,495), and shutouts (15). He was inducted into the Hall of Fame in 2019, less than two years after his death in an aviation accident.

MARCUS STROMAN, RHP (2014–2019)

"Height doesn't measure heart" is the mantra of the 5-foot-7 Stroman, who was drafted 22nd overall out of Duke by the Blue Jays in 2012. After a strong rookie showing in 2014, Stroman tore the ACL in his left knee during pitchers' fielding practice in the spring of 2015 but battled back to make four strong starts down the stretch, all Toronto wins, to help the Jays reach the postseason for the first time in 22 years. Healthy again in 2016, he topped 200 innings, then had a breakout year in 2017, posting a 3.09 ERA (145 ERA+) in 201 frames, finishing eighth in the Cy Young voting, and winning a Gold Glove (the fielding practice paid off, after all). Shoulder fatigue and a blister ruined his follow-up, and, after a dazzling start to the 2019 season, which included his first All-Star appearance, the Jays traded him to the Mets at the deadline.

A Taxonomy of 2020 Abnormalities

by Rob Mains

I'm going to start this with a trivia question. Trust me, it's relevant. Don't bother skipping to the end of the article to find the answer, it's not there.

Only five players have appeared in 140 or more games for 16 straight seasons. Who are they?

It's a trivia question starting off an essay, so you know how this works: Whatever you guessed, you're wrong. It's okay. As someone who purchased this book, chances are good that you're an educated baseball fan. But the circumstances behind 2020 force us to abandon, or at least seriously question, some of our favorite patterns and crutches for evaluating the game we love.

We just completed what was undoubtedly the strangest season in MLB history. No fans, geographically limited schedule, universal DH, seven-inning twin bills, runners on second in extra innings, a 16-team postseason, a club playing at a Triple-A stadium. Some of these changes will likely persist (sorry), but we've never had so many tweaks dumped on us all at once, at least not since they figured out how many balls were in a walk.

And the biggest, of course, was the 60-game season. The 19th century was dotted with teams that went bankrupt before the season ended, but the lone season with only 60 scheduled games was 1877. That year there were only six teams, the league rostered a total of 77 players (just 16 more than the 2020 Marlins), and batters called for pitches to be thrown high or low by the pitcher, who was 50 feet away. We can say the 2020 season was easily the shortest ever for recognizable baseball.

As such, it'll stand out. Few abbreviated seasons do. Just about everybody reading this knows the 1994 season ended after Seattle's Randy Johnson struck out Oakland's Ernie Young for the last out of the Mariners-A's game on August 11. The ensuing player strike wiped out the rest of the season and the postseason. Teams played only 112-117 games that year.

And many of you know that a strike in the middle of the 1981 season split the season in two, resulting in the only Division Series until 1995. Teams played only 103-111 games that year, the shortest regular season since 1885.

Those two seasons are memorable. So when we see that nobody drove in 100 runs in 1981, or that Greg Maddux was the only pitcher with 180 or more innings pitched in 1994, we think, "Of course. Strike year."

But we don't remember other short years. You might not recall that the 1994 strike spilled into the next year, chopping 18 games off the 1995 schedule. You might've read that the 1918 season, played during the last pandemic, ended after Labor Day due to the government's World War I "work or fight" order. A strike erased the first week and a half of the 1972 season, but that year's best known as the last time pitchers batted in the American League.

The point is, while we don't remember small changes to the schedule, we remember the big ones. The 1981 mid-season strike. The 1994 season- and Series-ending strike. And, of course, the pandemic-shortened 2020 season. We won't need a reminder why Marcell Ozuna's 18 homers were the fewest to lead the National League in a century. (Literally; Cy Williams led with 15 in 1920.)

Now, about that trivia question. The five players are Hank Aaron, Brooks Robinson, Pete Rose, Ichiro Suzuki, and Johnny Damon. The one nobody gets, of course, is Damon, and a lot of people miss Ichiro, whose last season of 140-plus games came garbed in the red-orange and ocean blue of Miami when he was 42. That's half of what makes it a good question. The other half is the two guys whom many think made the list but didn't. Lou Gehrig? His streak started in the Yankees' 42nd game of the 1925 season and lasted only 13 seasons after that. And everybody assumes Cal Ripken Jr. did it, having played 2,632 straight games over 17 seasons. But one of those 17 seasons was 1994, when the Orioles played only 112 games.

My point? *I just told you* everybody remembers the 1994 strike year, but everybody forgets it fell in the middle of Ripken's streak, separating the first twelve years from the last four. Just because we recall something doesn't mean it's always at the front of our minds.

Nobody is going to forget 2020, and baseball is obviously not the main reason. But there will come a time in the future when you're looking at a player's or a team's record, and there will be baffling numbers there for 2020, and you'll think, "I wonder what happened." (Not to mention the missing line for minor league players.) Just like you forgot that the 1994 strike limited Ripken to 112 games.

Try not to forget it, though. The 2020 season resulted in weird statistical results for several reasons.

There were only 60 games.
I know, duh. But that had impacts beyond counting stats like Ozuna's home run total or Yu Darvish and Shane Bieber leading the majors with eight wins. (I know, pitcher wins, but still.)

The 162-game season is the longest among major North American sports, and that duration gives us a gift. Over the course of a long season, small variations tend to even out. A player who has a ten-game hot streak will probably have a ten-game cold streak. A team that starts the year losing a bunch of close games will probably win a bunch of them. We get regression to the mean. Statistics stabilize.

Consider flipping a coin. Over the long run, we expect it to come up heads about half the time. But the fewer flips, the more variation there'll be. If you flip a coin six times, probability theory tells us you'll get at least two-third heads about 34 percent of the time. Flip it 30 times, your chance of two-thirds heads drops to five percent.

Or, relevant to this case, if you flip a coin 60 times, your chance of getting at least 36 heads—that's 60 percent—is 7.75 percent. Expand the coin-flipping to 162 times, and the chance of getting 60 percent heads drops to 0.73 percent.

In other words, the odds of an outcome that's 20 percent better (or worse) than expected is *more than ten times higher* when you flip your coin 60 times than when you do it 162 times. Call it small sample size, call lack of mean reversion, or call it luck not evening out, 162 is a lot more predictive than 60. You get much more variation over 60 games than over 162. Bieber's 1.63 ERA and 0.87 FIP aren't something we'd see over a full season, and neither is Javier Baéz's .203/.238/.360.

Some players' lines in 2020 look normal. Brian Anderson had an .811 OPS in 2019 and an .810 OPS in 2020. (He probably would have gotten that last point if he'd been given enough time.) But there are many like Bieber and Baéz, some of them from young players still establishing their talent levels. The answer to the question, "What went right or wrong for that guy in 2020?" is most likely "Nothing, it was just a 2020 thing."

Preseason training was abbreviated for hitters.

Every year, spring training drags. Players get tired of it, fans get tired of it, and you sure can tell sportswriters get tired of it. Yes, something to get everyone into shape is necessary, but does it really have to drag on for over a month? Can't we shorten it?

The 2020 season answered in the negative, at least for hitters. Warren Spahn is credited with saying that hitting is timing and pitching is upsetting timing. It appears nobody had his timing down after the abbreviated July summer camp. Through August 9—18 games into the season—MLB batters were hitting .230/.311/.395 with a .275 BABIP. That BABIP, had it held, would have been the lowest since 1968, the Year of the Pitcher. In recent years it's hovered around .300.

It didn't hold. Play returned to more normal levels the rest of the year: .249/.325/.425 with a .297 BABIP starting August 10. But batters whose play concentrated in those first two weeks wound up with ugly lines. Andrew

Benintendi went on the injured list with a season-ending rib cage strain on August 11. His final line: .103/.314/.128 in 14 games. Franchy Cordero went on the IL with a hamate bone fracture on August 9 and a .154/.185/.231 line. Even though he came back strong in a late September return, it was too late to repair his full-season numbers.

Preseason training was abbreviated for pitchers.

Every year, spring training drags. Players get tired of it, fans get tired of it ... wait, I already said that. But the abbreviated preseason was tough on pitchers, too. As noted, they had the upper hand coming out of the gate. But then they lost that hand. And then their arms, too.

The 2020 season was spread over 67 days. During those 67 days, 237 pitchers hit the Injured List, compared to 135 in the first 67 days of 2019. A lot of those IL stints, though, were COVID-19-related. Still, over the first 67 days of the 2019 season, there were 72 pitchers on the IL with arm injuries. That figure jumped to 110 in 2020, a 53 percent increase.

There are a number of factors contributing to pitcher arm injuries, ranging from usage to velocity, but it appears that attenuated preseason training played a role. A lot of pitchers had super-short seasons due to arm woes. Corey Kluber, Roberto Osuna, and Shohei Ohtani combined for seven innings, none after August 8. All suffered arm injuries. We'll never know whether they'd have fared better with a longer preseason, but we can guess how they probably feel.

Everybody played.

Rosters were set to expand from 25 to 26 in 2020, so even if we'd had a normal season, we'd have likely seen 2019's record of 1,410 players on MLB rosters broken. But due to the pandemic, rosters started the year at 30 and were cut to only 28. Add multiple COVID-19 absences and the revolving door caused by poor starts by hitters and a rash of pitcher arm injuries, and 1,289 players appeared in MLB games in 2020. The comparable figure over the first 67 days of the 2019 season was 1,109. That 16 percent increase works out to an average of six more players per team in 2020 compared to a similar slice of 2019. A future look back at 2020 rosters will include a lot of unfamiliar names.

Plus became a minus.

In advanced metrics, we adjust batter and pitcher performance for park and league/era variations. A plus sign appended to the end of a measure means that it's adjusted for park and league. It's scaled to an average of 100, with higher figures above average and lower figures below average. (Similarly, a metric with a minus is also park- and league-adjusted and scaled to 100, with lower values better.) Here at BP, our advanced measure of offensive performance is DRC+. Baseball-Reference has OPS+ and FanGraphs has wRC+.

Using park and league adjustments, we can compare Dante Bichette's 1995 Steroid Era season at pre-humidor Coors Field (.340/.364/.620, 40 homers, 128 RBI, MVP runner-up) with Jim Wynn's 1968 Year of the Pitcher season at the cavernous Astrodome (.269/.376/.474, 26 homers, 67 RBI, no MVP votes). It's not close. DRC+, OPS+, and wRC+ all give the nod to Wynn, handily. This is a useful tool. As my Baseball Prospectus colleague Patrick Dubuque tweeted last fall, "Please note that when I ask how you are, I am already adjusting for era."

The 2020 season messes up plus (and minus) stats for two reasons. First, the park adjustment was based on only 30 home games instead of the usual 81. Everything noted above regarding the short season applies, literally doubly, to park effect calculations. DRC+ uses a single-season park factor. OPS+ uses a three-year average and wRC+ five years. The figure for 2020 is suspect.

Second, OPS+ and wRC+ adjust for league: American and National. (DRC+ adjusts for opponent, regardless of league.) While there were two leagues in 2020, they were an artificial construct. To reduce travel, teams played opponents geographically, not based on league. There weren't two leagues, American and National. There were three, Western, Central, and Eastern.

That makes a difference because teams in the same league played in different run-scoring environments. AL teams scored 4.58 runs per game, NL teams 4.71. That's a small difference. But teams in the East scored 0.21 more runs per game (4.95) than teams in the West (4.74), and they both scored a lot more than Central teams (4.25). Adjusting for league misses that difference, so this book will be safe in that regard, but other sources may be distorted somewhat.

Not every game was a "game."
In 2020, the rising tide of strikeouts was finally stemmed. Strikeouts per team per game fell from 8.8 in 2019 to 8.7 in 2020. That marked the first decline after 14 straight annual increases.

In 2020, the rising tide of strikeouts rose higher. Batters struck out in 23.4 percent of plate appearances compared to 23.0 percent in 2019. That marked the 15th straight annual increase.

Both are true statements.

Because of two rule changes—seven-inning doubleheaders and runners on second in extra innings—games in 2020 were unprecedented in their brevity. There were 37.0 plate appearances per game in 2020. The only years with fewer were 1904 and 1906-1909. The average game in 2020 entailed 8.61 innings pitched, the fewest since 1899.

So when you see any per-game stats for 2020, you need to increase them by 3 or 4 percent to get them on equal footing with recent years.

Or, better, just ignore them. Last year happened. There were major league games contested between major league teams. But when you're looking at those physical or electronic baseball cards, when you're weaving narratives over why this young player's inevitable rise to stardom fell apart or why that old veteran rekindled his magic, don't linger on the 2020 line. It was just too weird. ■

Thanks to Lucas Apostoleris for research assistance.

—Rob Mains is an author of Baseball Prospectus.

Tranches of WAR

by Russell A. Carleton

We ask "replacement level" to be a lot of things. Sometimes contradictory things. Sometimes I wonder if we know what it even means anymore. The original idea was that it represented the level of production that a team could expect to get from "freely available talent", including bench players, minor leaguers, and waiver wire pickups. It created a common benchmark to compare everyone to, and for that reason, it represented an advancement well beyond what was available at the time. In fact, it created a language and a framework for evaluating players that was not just better but *entirely* different than what came before it.

But then we started mumbling in that language. The idea behind "wins above replacement" was one part sci-fi episode and one part mathematical exercise. Imagine that a player had disappeared before the season and suddenly, in an alternate timeline, his team would have had to replace him. The distance between him and that replacement line was his value. We need to talk about that alternate timeline.

Without getting too into 2:00 am "deep conversations" with extensive navel-gazing, it's worth thinking about why one player might not be playing, while another might.

- A player might not be playing because he has a short-term injury or his manager believes that he needs a day off.
- A player might not be playing because he has a longer-term injury that requires him to be on the injured list.

There's a difference here between these two situations. In particular, the first one generally *doesn't* involve a compensatory roster move, while the second one does. It's possible, though not guaranteed, that the person who will be replacing the injured/resting player would be the same in either case. That matters. Teams generally carry a spare part for all eight position players on the diamond, although in the era of a four-player bench, those spare parts usually are the backup plan for more than one spot.

131

A couple of years ago, I posed a hypothetical question. Suppose that a team had two players in its system fighting for a fourth outfielder spot. One of them was a league average hitter, but would be worth 20 runs below average if allowed to play center field for a full season. One of them was a perfectly average fielder, but would be 15 runs below average as a hitter, if allowed to play an entire season. Which of the two should the team roster? It's tempting to say the second one, as overall, he is the better player. That misses the point. A league average hitter on the bench isn't just a potential replacement for an injured outfielder. He might also pinch hit for the light-hitting shortstop in a key spot. You keep the average hitter on the roster, even though he isn't a hand-in-glove fit for one specific place on the field, because being a bench player is a different job description than being a long-term fill-in for someone. If you find yourself in need of a longer-term fill-in, you can bring the other guy up from AAA.

When we're determining the value of an everyday player though, if he had disappeared before the season and a team would have had to replace his production, they likely would have done it with a player who was a long-term fill-in type because they would have had to replace a guy who played everyday. Maybe that's the same guy that they would have rostered on their bench anyway, but we don't know. It gets to the query of what we hope to accomplish with WAR. Are we looking for an accurate modeling of reality or are we looking for a common baseline to compare everyone to? Both have their uses, but they are somewhat different questions.

Let's talk about another dichotomy.

- A player might not be playing because he isn't very good and is a bench-level player.
- A player might not be playing because there is another player on the team who has a situational advantage that makes him the better choice today. The classic case of this is a handedness platoon. On another day, he might be a better choice.

When we think about player usage, I think we're still stuck in the model that there are starters and there are scrubs. We have plenty of words for bench players or reserves or backups or utility guys. We do still have the word "platoon" in our collective vocabulary, but in the age of short benches, it's hard to construct one. It's always been hard to construct them. You have to find two players who hit with different hands, have skill sets that complement each other, and probably play the same position. In the era of the short bench, one of them had probably better double as a utility player in some way. Baseball has a two-tiered language geared toward the idea of regulars and reserves. The fact that it was so easy for me to find plenty of synonyms for "a player whose primary function is to come into a game to replace a regular player if he is injured or resting" should tell you something.

I'm always one to look for "unspoken words" in baseball. What is it called when someone is both half of a platoon and the utility infielder? That guy exists sometimes, but he reveals himself in that role—usually by accident. We don't have a word for that, and whenever I find myself saying "we don't have a word for that", I look for new opportunities. What do you call it, further, when the job of being the utility infielder is decentralized across the whole infield with occasional contributions from the left fielder? It's not even a "super-utility" player. What happens when you build your entire roster around the idea that everyone will be expected to be a triple major?

⚾   ⚾   ⚾

I think someone else beat me to this one, and on a grand scale. Platoons work because we know that hitters of the opposite hand to the pitcher get better results than hitters of the same hand, usually to the tune of about 20 points of OBP. If you want to express that in runs, it usually comes out to somewhere around 10 to 12 runs of linear weights value prorated across 650 PA. But hang on a second, now let's say that we have two players who might start today, both of roughly equal merit with the bat. One has a handedness advantage, but is the worse fielder of the two. In that case, as long as his "over the course of a season" projection as a fielder at whatever position you want to slot him into is less than a 10-run drop from the guy he might replace, then he's a better option today.

We're not used to thinking of utility players as bat-first options, who would play below-average defense at three different infield positions. That guy might hook on as a 2B/3B/LF type (Howie Kendrick, come on down!) but teams usually think to themselves that they need as their utility infielder someone who "can handle" shortstop, the toughest of the infield spots to play. If someone can do that *and* hit well, he's probably already starting somewhere, so he's not available as a utility infielder. It's easier for those glove guys to find a job. In a world where the replacement for a shortstop *has to be* the designated utility infielder, that makes sense.

But as we talked about last week, we're living in a different world. The rate at which a replacement for a regular starter turns out to be *another starter* shifting over to cover has gone way up over the last five years. There was always some of it in the game, but this has been a supernova of switcheroos. Now if your second baseman is capable of playing a decent shortstop, that 2B/3B/LF guy can swap in. He's not actually playing shortstop, and maybe the defense suffers from the switch, but if he's got enough of a bat, he might outhit those extra fielding miscues. And in doing so, he is effectively your backup shortstop.

Somewhere along the lines, teams got hip to the idea of multi-positional play from their regulars. I've written before about how you can't just put a player, however athletic, into a new position and expect much at first. The data tell us that. Eventually, players can learn to be multi-positionalists, but it takes time, roughly on the order of two months, before they're OK. But there's a hidden message in there. If you give a player some reps at a new spot, he's a reasonably gifted athlete and somewhat smart and willing to learn, he could probably pick it up enough to get to "good enough," and it doesn't take forever. You just have to be purposeful about it. Maybe you get to the point where you can start to say "he's still below average but we could move him there and get another bat into the lineup, and it's a net win."

Teams have started to build those extra lessons into their player development program. It used to be seen as a mark of weakness to be relegated to "utility player" because that meant that you were a bench player (all those synonyms above come with a side of stigma). Now, it's a way of building a team. If you get a few reps in the minors (where it doesn't count) at a spot, you'll have at least played the spot at game speed before. There are limits to how far you can push that. A slow-footed "he's out in left field because we don't have the DH" guy is never going to play short, but maybe your third baseman can try second base and not look like a total moose out there.

⚾   ⚾   ⚾

Back to WAR. I'd argue that the world of starters and scrubs is slowly disintegrating, for good cause. In the event that a regular starter really does go down with an injury–ostensibly, the alternate universe scenario that WAR is attempting to model–it makes the team a little more resilient to replacing him. And the good news is that you're more likely to be able to replace him with the best of the bench bunch, rather than the third-best guy, because the best guy doesn't have to be an exact positional match for the guy who got hurt. And that's what the manager would want to do. He'd want to replace that long-term production, not with an amalgam of everyone else who played that position, but with the best guy available from his reserves.

Now this is still WAR. We still want to retain the principle that we should be measuring a player, and not his teammates. We need some sort of common baseline, and despite what I just said, we'll still need some sort of amalgam. To construct that, I give to you the idea of the tranche. The word, if you've not heard it before, refers to a piece of a whole that is somehow segmented off. It's often used in finance to talk about layers of a financial instrument.

Here, I want you to consider that there are 30 starters at each of the seven non-battery positions (catchers should have their own WAR, since only a catcher can replace a catcher). We can identify them by playing time, and we can futz around with the definition a little bit if we need to. Next, among those who aren't in that starting pool, we identify the top tranche of the 30 best bench players, which I would again identify by playing time, and then the second and third and fourth and so on. If a player were to disappear, his manager would probably want to take a guy from that top tranche of the bench to replace him. In a world where even the starters can slide around the field, that becomes more feasible.

We can take a look at that top tranche and say "How many of them showed that they are able to play (first, second, etc.)?" and therefore could have directly substituted for the starter? How many of them could have been a direct substitute for our injured player? We don't know whether one of them would be on *a specific* team, but we can say that 40 percent of the time, a manager would have been able to draw from tranche 1 in filling the role, and 35 percent from tranche 2. But on tranche 1, we can also look at how many of those players played a position that could have then shifted and covered for that spot. We'd need some eligibility criteria for all of this (probably a minimum number of games played) but it would just be a matter of multiplication. Shortstop would be harder to fill, and managers would probably be dipping a little further down in the talent pool, and so replacement level would be lower, as it is now.

Doing some quick analysis, I found that the difference in just batting linear weights (haven't even gotten into running or fielding) between tranche 1 and tranche 2 in 2019 was about 6.5 runs, prorated across 650 PA. Between tranche 1 and tranche 3, it's 10.8 runs. The ability to shift those plate appearances up the ladder has some real value.

This part is important. We can also give credit to starters for the positions that they showed an ability to play, even if they didn't play them (this is the guy fully capable of playing center, but who's in a corner because the team already has a good center fielder) because he allows a team to carry a player who hits like a left fielder to functionally be the team's backup center fielder. He facilitates that movement upward among the tranches. We can start to appreciate the difference between a left fielder who would never be able to hack it in center (and the compensatory move that his team would have to make) and the left fielder who could do it, but just didn't have to very often.

Past that, you can continue to use whatever hitting and fielding and running metrics you like to determine a player's value, but when we get down to constructing that baseline, I'd argue we need a better conceptual and mathematical framework. It's going to require some more #GoryMath than we're used to, but I'd argue it's a better conceptualization of the way that MLB actually plays the game in 2020. If…y'know…MLB plays in 2020. If WAR is going to be our flagship statistic among the *acronymati*, then we need to acknowledge that it contains some old and starting-to-be-out-of-date assumptions about the game. We may need to tinker with it. Here's my idea for how. ▪

—*Russell A. Carleton is an author of Baseball Prospectus.*

Secondhand Sport

by Patrick Dubuque

Back before time stopped, I liked to go to thrift stores. Now that I'm older, I rarely ever buy anything—I don't need much in my life, now—but I still enjoy the old familiar circuit: check to see if there are baseball cards to write about, look for board or card games to play with the kids, scan for random ironic jerseys, hit the book section. It takes ten, maybe fifteen minutes. Thrift stores are the antithesis of modern online shopping, because you don't know what they have, and you don't even really know what you want. It's junk, literal junk, stuff other people thought was worthless. That's what makes it great.

In an idealized economy, thrift stores shouldn't exist. Everybody has a living wage, and every product has a durability that exactly matches its desired life; nothing should need to be given away, no one should need to be given to. But then, thrift stores shouldn't work on a customer experience level, either. You wouldn't think an ethos of "let's make everything disorganized and hard to find" would lead to customer satisfaction, but low-budget retailers like TJ Maxx and Ross thrive on this model. People like bargain hunting as much for the hunting as the bargain; it's part of the experience, spending time as if it's a wager. There's a thrill, occasionally, in inefficiency.

In sports, the modern overuse of the word "inefficiency" is a condemnation: It insinuates that there is *an* efficiency, a correct way to be found, and that all other ways are wrong ways. It's prevalent in baseball but hardly contained to it; the lifehack, the Silicon Valley disruption are other examples of productivity creep in our daily lives. Their modern success makes plenty of sense. Maximization of resources, after all, is its own puzzle, and an industry of European board games is founded upon it. It's fun to take a system and optimize it, unravel it like a sudoku puzzle. If there's only one kind of genius, after all, there's no way anyone can fail to appreciate it.

Baseball has been hacking away at these perceived inefficiencies since its inception: platoons, bullpens, farm systems were all installed to extract more out of the tools at hand. But it's been a particular badge of the sabermetric movement, from Ken Phelps and his All-Star Team to Ricardo Rincon and the darlings of *Moneyball*. It's business, but it's also an ethos: the idea that there's treasure among the trash, something we all failed to appreciate until someone brought it to light.

It's the myth that made Sidd Finch so enticing, that fuels so many "best shape" narratives and new pitch promises. We all, athletes and unathletic sportswriters, want to believe that there's genius trapped inside us, and that it's just a matter of puzzling out the combination to unlock it. That our art, our style is the next inefficiency, waiting for our own Billy Beane. It's why we root for underdogs, and why we're excited for the Mike Tauchmans and the Eurubiel Durazos, champions of skin-deep mediocrity.

Except we aren't anymore, really. The days of "Free X" have descended beyond the ring of irony and into obscurity. There are still Xs to be freed, or at least one X, duplicated endlessly: Mike Ford, Luke Voit, Max Muncy. The undervalued one-dimensional slugger demonstrated how the game hasn't quite culturally caught up to its logical extreme. But for those who don't fit the rather spacious mold, times are grimmer. As Rob Arthur revealed several months ago, there's been a marked increase in the number of sub-replacement relievers. It's the outcome of a greater number of teams forced to play out games without the talent to win them, but it's also emblematic of the modern tendency of teams to dispose of their disposable assets, burning through cost-controlled arms the way that man chopped down forests in *The Lorax*. Stuff just isn't built to outlive their original owners anymore.

It's unsurprising, given how well-mined the market for inefficiencies has been of late. The disciples of the early analytics departments, and the disciples of those, have proliferated the league, with only a few backwater holdouts. The league has grown smarter, but every team has learned the same lesson. In fact, the phenomenon creates a peculiar kind of feedback loop: As teams value a specific subset of players or skills, prospective athletes learn to increase their own marketability by conforming themselves to the demands of their prospective employers.

And that's tragic, in the way that the extinction of animals is tragic; a certain amount of biodiversity in baseball has been lost. Shortstops hit like outfielders. Pitchers don't hit at all. Only the catchers remain idiosyncratic, thanks to the defensive demands of their position; eventually they too will be required to produce like everyone else, or they'll meet the fate of their battery mates. A perfect economy requires perfect production.

I mentioned earlier that more and more, I leave thrift stores empty-handed. It is true that I am more discerning than in the past; my bookshelves are full, and there are more streaming films than I will ever be able to watch. But there are other factors at play.

Thrift stores are, in a way, the bond markets of retail. When the economy is rough and other retailers are struggling, more people look secondhand for their products. But as recently as last year, publications were noting a reversal of the trend: Companies like Goodwill and Savers were expanding despite a strong economy. Publications credited a heightened sense of environmentalism and a rejection of cutting-edge fashion as drivers behind the increase, though the more likely answer is the modern American economy hasn't showered its favors equally, particularly among the young.

But it is more than just the economy. Baseball and thrift stores share something else in common, evident in our current conversations about re-starting the sport: They live in the gray area between public service and private enterprise. Thrift stores provide affordable necessities to lower-class citizens, and collectibles and fashion for the middle-class. Because of the success of the latter, prices have gone up across the board. Especially in terms of clothing, the middle-class flight from fashion into vintage has instead carried the aftereffects of fashion, including its costs, into a territory where people just want clothes. But there's another factor in the rise of prices, in the form of the internet.

The Goodwills of the world have grown smarter, too, employing the internet to extract full value from their detritus. Ebay, similarly, has lost much of the charm it had as a new frontier around the turn of the century. Everything has a price point now; even individual taste is no match for the algorithm, because anything rare, no matter how niche its market, is a collectible to someone.

The internet has had the same effect on thrift stores that sabermetrics has had on baseball; its equivalent to OBP was the bar scanner. As detailed in Slate, the rise of second-party stores on eBay and Amazon birthed an entire industry of used-good salespeople, armed with PDAs and scanners, buying books for three dollars to sell online for five. The author, Michael Savitz, reports earning $60,000 by working nearly 80 hours a week; he makes it clear that this is not a vocation of his choosing. It's long hours, with no real creativity or individuality, skimming the cream off of a local establishment and flipping it to someone with a little more money on the other side of the country. And once the vocation exists, the obvious question arises: why wait to put the wares out on the shelves? Why allow value to exist at all?

Nothing is ruined. Thrift stores will continue to sell polo shirts and DVDs, and baseball will continue to exist and make or lose money, depending on who you believe. But as we continue to refine our knowledge, we lose something in the conquest for efficiency, a delight born out of the unknown. The problem isn't the efficiency itself; we can't blame the booksellers, or the people sweeping freeways to collect grams of platinum from damaged catalytic converters. The problem is a system that requires this sort of profit-skimming behavior in order to feed families (or, for corporations, maximize shareholder return).

In times like these, with the 2020 season on the brink and the collective bargaining agreement close behind, it can often feel like the current situation is untenable. It can't keep going like this, even if we don't know what to do about it. But as with thrift stores, there's an equally irresistible feeling that it *has* to keep going, that it would be unimaginable to not have this broken, amazing sport. Both industries exist on an invisible foundation of friction, of chaos and unpredictability, even as both see their foundations buffed down to a perfect, untouchable polish. But if COVID-19 and its financial ramifications do, as some have suggested, make it such that the baseball that returns is fundamentally different than the baseball that came before, perhaps this is the time to lean in, and change the game even more. Fix bunting. Make defense more difficult. Create viable, alternate strategies. Add some chaos back into baseball. It's fun when no one knows quite where things are.

—Patrick Dubuque is an author of Baseball Prospectus.

Steve Dalkowski Dreaming

by Steven Goldman

We dream of being a pitcher, of starring in the major leagues. Depending on your age and your sense of historical perspective, you might imagine yourself as Walter Johnson, throwing harder than anyone else—hitting more batters than anyone else, too, but always feeling bad about it. You could picture yourself as a Tom Seaver or a David Cone, with all the stuff in the world but still being cerebral about it, thinking about so much more than burning 'em in there. There are so many models one could choose: You could be a Lefty Gomez, Jim Bouton, or Bill Lee, skilled, but not taking the whole thing too seriously, or a Lefty Grove, Bob Gibson, or Steve Carlton, powerful but treating each start like a mission to be survived instead of a game to be enjoyed.

Very few would dream of being Steve Dalkowski, the former Baltimore Orioles prospect who died of COVID-19 last week at the age of 80. Yet, there is something just as noble in Dalkowski's negative accomplishments—and accomplishments is what they are—as there is in the precision-engineered pitching of a Greg Maddux. You have to be very good to be that bad. Dalkowski had all of the stuff of the greatest pitchers but none of the command; his story is not one of failing to conquer his limitations, but striving against one of the cruelest hands that fate or genetics or personality can deal us: A desire to achieve great things which is almost but not quite matched by the ability to meet that goal.

As with Johnson, Grove, Bob Feller, and the rest of the hard-throwing pitchers who played before the advent of modern radar guns, we have to take the word of the players and coaches who saw Dalkowski pitch as to his velocity. He was a hard-drinking, maximum-effort pitcher who, if their memories are to be believed, consistently threw over 100 miles per hour. His was the Maltese Fastball, the stuff that dreams are made of. The problem is that velocity without command and control is still a good distance from utility. Dalkowski was the most effective towel you could design for a fish, the sleekest bathing suit intended to be worn by an astronaut, but that doesn't mean he wasn't beautiful: We can appreciate a journey even if it doesn't end at the intended destination.

141

Whether because of sloppy mechanics he couldn't calm, an inability to understand that a consistent 98 in the strike zone would likely be more effective than a consistent 110 out of it, or all that beer, Dalkowski could never make the adjustments that pitchers like Feller and Nolan Ryan made before him, possibly because he had so far to go: Feller, who never pitched in the minors, came up at 17 and spent three years walking almost seven batters per nine innings before settling in at 3.8 beginning when he was 20. Ryan started out walking over six batters per nine but gradually improved as his long career played out; for him to go from 6.2 walks per nine with the 1966 Greenville Mets to 3.7 with the 1989 Texas Rangers represents a 40 percent reduction. An equivalent improvement by Dalkowski would still have left him walking over 11 batters per nine innings.

Dalkowski was like *The Room* of pitchers, a player so bad he became good again. Cal Ripken, Sr., who both played with and managed Dalkowski, recalled in a 1979 *Sporting News* "where are they now" piece the occasion when the pitcher crossed up his catcher and his fastball, "hit the plate umpire smack in the mask. The mask broke all to pieces and the umpire wound up in the hospital for three days with a concussion. If they ever had a radar gun in those days, I'll bet Dalkowski would have been timed at 110 miles an hour."

Signed by the Orioles out of New Britain High in Connecticut in 1957, Dalkowski was sent to Kingsport in the Appalachian League, where he pitched 62 innings. He allowed only 22 hits in 62 innings, or 3.2 per nine, a number with no equivalent in major league history (though Aroldis Chapman came close in 2014), and also struck out 121 (17.6 per nine) and walked 129 (18.7). He was also charged with 39 wild pitches. That June, one of his fastballs clipped a Dodgers prospect named Bob Beavers and carried away part of his ear. "The first pitch was over the backstop, the second pitch was called a strike, I didn't think it was," Beavers said last year. "The third pitch hit me and knocked me out, so I don't remember much after that. I couldn't get in the sun for a while, and I never did play baseball again." Former minor leaguer Ron Shelton based the *Bull Durham* pitcher Nuke LaLoosh on Dalkowski. And yet, to see him as a figure of fun, an amusing loser, is to misunderstand something unique and strange.

Dalkowski kept on posting some of the strangest lines in baseball history. Pitching for the Stockton Ports of the Class C California League in 1960, he struck out 262 and walked 262 in 170 innings. Yet, he did improve, especially after pitching for Earl Weaver at Elmira in 1962. Weaver had previously had Dalkowski at Aberdeen in 1959, but wasn't ready to grapple with him then. This time he was. "I had grown more and more concerned about players with great physical abilities who could not learn to correct certain basic deficiencies no matter how much you instructed or drilled them," he related in his autobiography, *It's What You Learn After You Know It All That Counts*. He got permission from the Orioles to give all of his players the Stanford-Binet IQ test. "Dalkowski finished in the 1 percentile in his ability to understand facts. Steve, it was said to say, had the ability to do everything but learn." [sic]

IQ tests are problematic diagnostic tools, so take Weaver's estimate of Dalkowski's mental capabilities with a grain of salt. What's important is that even if he got to the right answer by way of the wrong reason, Weaver had learned something valuable. His insight was to stop asking Dalkowski to learn new pitches and just let him get by with the two that he had. Were Dalkowski a prospect today, that would have been a no-brainer: Can't develop a third pitch? The bullpen is right over there, sir. Player development wasn't like that then, but Weaver, temporarily Dalkowski's mentor, could let him work with what he had. According to Weaver, the pitcher responded: "In the final 57 innings he pitched that season Dalkowski gave up 1 earned run, struck out 110 batters, and walked only 11." It's not true—as per the *Elmira Star-Gazette*, as of late July, Dalkowski had walked 71 in 106 innings and finished with 114 in 160 innings, which means Dalkowski's control actually faded at the end of the season rather than improved—but that doesn't mean it didn't happen in some sense, just that it didn't happen that way. Again, it's the journey, not the destination, and his ERA was 3.04 so *something* had gone right.

Also along the way: The next spring, Orioles manager Billy Hitchcock was rooting for Dalkowski to make the team as a long-man—maybe Weaver had gotten through to him. There were things out of Weaver's control, like the universe's twisted sense of humor: that March, Dalkowski's elbow went "twang."

You sometimes read that it was the Orioles' insistence on Dalkowski learning the curve that did him in, but even if they hadn't learned their lesson, the injury was probably just a coincidence: Dalkowski had thrown an incredible number of pitches over the previous few years. Still, it testifies to the dangers of trying to get what you want and risking the loss of what you had. Dalkowski tried to come back, but the 110-mph stuff was gone. A pitcher with no control and no stuff is...a civilian. What followed were years of vagabond living, arrests for drunkenness. There were Alcoholics Anonymous meetings, assistance from baseball alumni associations, but none of it took. From the 1990s until the time of his passing he dwelt in an assisted living facility, suffering from alcohol-related dementia. He'd been a heavy drinker since his teenage years. As with all those pitches per game, there was a price to be paid. You make choices on the journey and some of them are irrevocable. It's like a fairy tale: "Bite of poison apple? Don't mind if I do."

In the aforementioned *Sporting News* profile, Chuck Stevens, the head of the Association of Professional Ballplayers of America, a ballplayer charity, said, "I've got nothing against drinking. I do it myself sometimes. But, I don't condone common drunkenness. We went through lots of heartache and many dollars, but Dalkowski didn't want to help himself and we weren't going to keep him drunk." The journey is *un*like a fairy tale: No one will come along and kiss it better, not if they're busy forming judgments.

In the end, we are left with a sort of philosophical chicken/egg conundrum: Is failing to meet your goals evidence of unfulfilled potential or the lack of it? Isn't what you did by definition what you were capable of doing? Or could you have broken through to something better with the right help, the right lucky break? These are unanswerable questions, and how we try to answer them may say more about us than about the people we're judging.

No pitcher ever has it easy. *All* pitchers must work hard. *All* pitchers must refine their craft. It's almost never just about *stuff*. Dalkowski dreaming is no insult to the great pitchers who made it; from Pete Alexander to Max Scherzer, they have all earned their way up. And yet, if it is true that we can only do as much as we can do, then the journey would be more of an adventure, the ultimate triumph or defeat more noble, if like Dalkowski we lacked 100 percent of the confidence, the command, the self-possession, the commitment, the resistance to making bad decisions that so many great players possess—to be gloriously human. Or, to put it more succinctly, it would be fun to be able to throw as hard as any person ever has. Even if just for a moment, and even if nothing more came of it than that, no one could say you hadn't lived life to the fullest. ∎

—Steven Goldman is an author of Baseball Prospectus.

A Reward For A Functioning Society

by Cory Frontin and Craig Goldstein

On July 5, Nationals reliever Sean Doolittle said in the middle of a press conference regarding the restart of Major League Baseball and what would later be known as summer camp, "sports are like the reward of a functioning society." This sentence was amidst a much longer, thoughtful reply about the societal and health conditions under which MLB players were being brought back. It's a very similar sentiment to one Jane McManus used on April 7, when she discussed the White House's meeting with sports commissioners. She said "sports are the effect of a functioning society—not the precursor."

Both versions of the same sentiment spoke to a laudable ideal in the context of a country that was not addressing a rampaging virus, and opting instead to bring sports back for the feeling of normalcy rather than the reality of it. "Priorities," as McManus said.

On Wednesday, the NBA's Milwaukee Bucks conducted a wildcat/political strike, refusing to come out for Game 5 of their playoff series against the Orlando Magic. The Magic refused to accept the forfeit, and shortly thereafter other playoff series were threatened by player strikes. Eventually the league moved to postpone that day's games, folding to players leveraging their united power.

The backdrop against which these actions took place was the shooting by police of Jacob Blake. Blake was shot in the back seven times by police, as he attempted to get into his vehicle. He managed to survive the assault, but is paralyzed from the waist down.

⚾　　　⚾　　　⚾

The step taken to walk out, first by the Milwaukee Bucks, then subsequently by other NBA, WNBA, and MLB teams, was a step toward upholding the virtue of the sentiment described by McManus and Doolittle. But that sentiment does not align with the broad history of sports in this and other countries, a history that contradicts the core of the idealistic statement.

Sports have been a significant part of American society for most of its existence, expanding in importance and influence in recent years. The idea that society was functioning in a way that was worthy of the reward of sports for most of that time is laughable. Much of America is not functioning and has not functioned for Black people, full stop. The oppressed people at the center of this political act by players, specifically Black players, in concert throughout the NBA and in fits and starts throughout Major League Baseball, have not known a society that functions for them rather than *because* of them.

Politics has been part of the sports landscape since the inception of sport, but for just about as long people have bemoaned its presence. Sports are to be an escape, it is said. An escape from what, though? A functioning society?

No, the presence of sports has never signified a cultural or political system that is on the up and up. Rather, the presence of sports *reflect and reinforce the society* that produces them.

⚾   ⚾   ⚾

The Negro Leagues were born out of societal dysfunction. The need for entirely separate leagues, composed of Black and Latino players barred from the Major Leagues because of racism? That is not a functioning society, and yet there were sports.

Even the integration of players from the Negro Leagues resulted in a transfer of power and wealth from Black-owned businesses and communities and into white ones, mirroring the dysfunction that had bled into every aspect of American society at the time. Japheth Knopp noted in the Spring 2016 Baseball Research Journal:

> The manner in which integration in baseball—and in American businesses generally—occurred was not the only model which was possible. It was likely not even the best approach available, but rather served the needs of those in already privileged positions who were able to control not only the manner in which desegregation occurred, but the public perception of it as well in order to exploit the situation for financial gain. Indeed, the very word integration may not be the most applicable in this context because what actually transpired was not so much the fair and equitable combination of two subcultures into one equal and more homogenous group, but rather the reluctant allowance—under certain preconditions—for African Americans to be assimilated into white society.

To understand the value of a movement, though, is not to understand how it is co-opted by ownership, but to know the people it brings together and what they demand. When Jackie Robinson—the player who demarcated the inevitability of the end of the Negro leagues—attended the March on Washington for Jobs and Freedom in 1963, he did so with his family and marched alongside the people. He stood alongside hundreds of thousands to fight for their common civil and labor rights. "The moral arc of the universe is long," many freedom fighters have echoed, "but it bends towards justice." The bend, it is less frequently said, happens when a great mass of people place the moral arc of the universe on their knee and apply force, as Jackie, his family, and thousands of others did that day.

⚾   ⚾   ⚾

Of course, taking the moral arc of the universe down from the mantle and bending it is not without risk. Perhaps the outsized influence of athletes is itself a mark of a dysfunctional society, but, nonetheless, hundreds of athletes woke up on Wednesday morning with the power to bring in millions of dollars in revenues. That very power, as we would come to find out, was matched with the equal and opposite power to *not* bring those revenues. That power, in hands ranging from the Milwaukee Bucks, to Kenny Smith in the *Inside the NBA* Studio, from the unexpected ally, Josh Hader, and his largely white teammates to the notably Black Seattle Mariners, would be exercised for a single demand: the end to state violence against Black people. Not unlike the March itself, it sat at the intersection of the civil rights of Black Americans and bold labor action. The March on Washington stood in the face of a false notion of integration—against an integration of extraction but not one of equality—and proposed something different. Just the same, the acts of solidarity of August 26, 2020 will be remembered in stark defiance of MLB's BLM-branded, but ultimately empty displays on opening weekend.

Bold defiance like this can never be without risk. By choosing to exercise this power, the Milwaukee Bucks took a risk. They risked vitriol and backlash from those they disagreed with. They risked fines or seeing their contracts voided, as a walkout like this is prohibited by their CBA. They risked forfeiting a playoff game, one that, as the No. 1 seed in the playoffs, they'd worked all year to attain. They didn't know how Orlando would respond. It wasn't clear that other teams throughout the league would follow suit in solidarity. And it wasn't known the league would accept these actions and moderately co-opt them by "postponing" games that would have featured no players.

If the league reschedules the games, some of the athletes' risk—their shared sacrifice—will be diminished, in retrospect. But they did not know any of that when they took that risk. And it is often left to athletes to take these risks when others in society won't, especially those of their same socioeconomic status and levels of influence.

It is athletes, specifically BIPOC athletes, that take them, though, because they live with the risk of being something other than white in this country every day. They are no strangers to the realities of police brutality. It seems incongruous then, to say that sports are a reward for a functioning society when we rely on athletes to lead us closer to being a functioning society. Luckily, our beloved athletes, WNBA players first and foremost among them, understand what sports truly are: a pipebender for the moral arc of the universe.

—Craig Goldstein is editor in chief of Baseball Prospectus. Cory Frontin is an author of Baseball Prospectus.

Index of Names

For the Joy of Keeping Score

THIRTY81 Project is an ongoing graphic design project focused on the ballparks of baseball. Since being established in 2013, scorecards have been a fundamental part of the effort. Each two-page card is uniquely ballpark-centric — there are 30 variants — and designed with both beginning and veteran scorekeepers in mind. Evolving over the years with suggestions from fans, broadcasters, and official scorers, the sheets are freely available to everyone as printable letter-size PDFs at the project webshop: www.THIRTY81Project.com

Download, Print, Score, Repeat ...

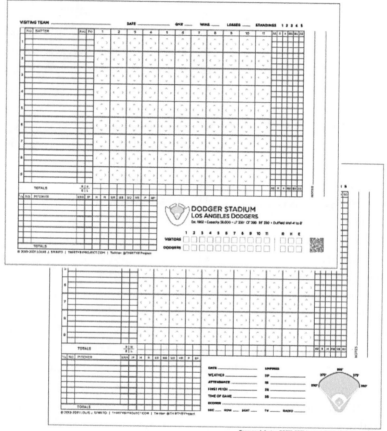

Scorecard design ©2013-2021 Louis J. Spirito | THIRTY81Project